M000074509

MASS COMMUNICATION LAW IN VIRGINIA

By W. Wat Hopkins

NEW FORUMS PRESS INC.

Stillwater, Oklahoma U.S.A.

This book may be ordered in bulk quantities at discount from New Forums Press, Inc., P.O. Box 876, Stillwater, OK 74076 [Federal I.D. No. 73 1123239]. Printed in the United States of America.

International Standard Book Number: 1-58107-047-0

Table of Contents

Mass Communication Law in Virginia

Preface

Since 1931, when the U.S. Supreme Court noted in *Gitlow v. New York* that the constitutional protections of free speech and press are applicable to the states through the Fourteenth Amendment, the Court has often waded into areas of mass communication law that had previously been left to the states. These days, therefore, the term "mass communication law" often evokes musings about constitutional law and landmark Supreme Court opinions like *Near v. Minnesota, New York Times Co. v. Sullivan, Miller v. California, Hustler v. Falwell* and *Texas v. Johnson.*

On the othr hand, the term "mass communication law" almost never causes reflection about state constitutions, state statutes and state supreme court rulings. And that's unfortunate, because much of the law of mass communication remains in the hands of state legislatures and courts. In matters involving libel, invasion of privacy, obscenity, prior restraint and access, individual states often have the final say. The law of mass communication, therefore, can vary considerably from state to state.

That's why this book is important. It's designed to explain those variations of the law as they exist in Virginia.

I should note that the name *Mass Communication Law in Virginia* is a bit misleading. Certainly, the book focuses primarily on law that relates to mass communication – there are chapters on libel, privacy, free press and fair trial, confidential sources, advertising and pornography. But the book goes beyond "mass communication law." Picketing and symbolic expression, for example, are not forms of mass communication law, but they are forms of speech, as that term has been defined by the U.S. Supreme Court and the Virginia Supreme Court. In addition, Virginia's freedom of information act is designed as a citizens' law, not a press law, though members of the press may use it more often than other citizens do. So "communication law" is covered here in addition to "mass communication law."

I hope the book has many readers, but I wrote it primarily to help three specific groups: college students studying journalism or communications in the commonwealth, professional journalists who need a reference book on state law as it applies to them, and high school journalists who are beginning to cope with the problems of free expression.

Writing the book was no easy job, but a number of people made it easier than it could have been. Professors around the state who teach communication law courses sent me helpful comments. I am particularly grateful to Teresa Keller of Emory and Henry College and Sam Riley, a colleague in the Department of Communication Studies at Virginia Tech. Bob Hughes, formerly of Virginia Commonwealth University; Alice Neff Lucan, who is associated with the law firm of Hudgins, Carter and Coleman in Alexandria, and Ginger Stanley, executive director of the Virginia Press Association, made many helpful comments on the first edition.

Frosty Landon, executive director of the Virginia Coalition for Open Government, Lawrence Hammack of *The Roanoke Times,* and Alan Cooper of *The Richmond Times-Dispatch,* provided information and comments on the second edition.

I am also grateful to the faculty of the Department of Communication Studies at Virginia Tech for creating an atmosphere that makes teaching and research a pleasure.

As always, I must thank my wife, Roselynn, for her continuous support. Without her I would be able to do very little work of any kind.

I hope you will let me know what's right and wrong with this book. There will be regular updates and, as always with law previous. I will, therefore, take each comment to heart as I continue my effort to keep track with the changes in communication law in the commonwealth. So please write or call:

W. Wat Hopkins
Department of Communication Studies - 0311
Virginia Tech
Blacksburg, VA 24061
(540) 231-9833
whopkins@vt.edu

For
Lincoln, Jonathan and Sam

Chapter 1

VIRGINIA'S FREE EXPRESSION HERITAGE

Virginia is sometimes called "Mother of Presidents," because eight of the nation's chief executive officers have come from the commonwealth.[1] Virginia might also be called the "Mother of the First Amendment," however, because its contributions to freedom of expression in the early United States are unmatched. For example:

- In 1776, Virginia became the first colony to establish legal protection for the press, a precursor to the First Amendment to the U.S. Constitution.
- Virginia's constitutional ratifying convention was the first among the states to propose that a clause ensuring press freedom be added to the Constitution.
- A Virginian, James Madison, introduced into the First Congress a document – which included two free expression provisions – that would be molded by legislative committees into the federal Bill of Rights.
- Virginia played a key role in the ratification of the Bill of Rights when, on December 15, 1791, it became the tenth

---

[1] Virginia's eight presidents are George Washington (1789-1897), Thomas Jefferson (1801-1809), James Madison (1809-1817), James Monroe (1818-1825), William Henry Harrison (1841), John Tyler (1841-1845), Zachary Taylor (1848-1850) and Woodrow Wilson (1913-1921).

state to ratify the document, ensuring that a free expression guarantee would become the law of the land.[2]

- The Virginia Resolutions, adopted during the controversy over the Sedition Act of 1798, were instrumental in the development of the concept that citizens have the right to criticize the government and government officials. The concept would become the cornerstone for free speech protection in the United States.[3]

Virginia, therefore, has displayed a distinguished role in the heritage of free expression – a heritage extended at least to the War for Independence, when press protection in Virginia got its first real foot-hold. During that war, Virginia became the first of eleven states to include a press protection clause in what was tantamount to a state constitution.[4]

The document was the Virginia Declaration of Rights and grew out of a series of conventions called by Virginia colonists to deal with the increasing tension between the colonies and England. Delegates to the fifth, and final, of these conventions adopted the Resolutions for Proposing Independence on May 15, 1776. The first resolution instructed Virginia's delegates to the Continental Congress to call for a declaration of independence from England.

The second resolution provided for the establishment of a committee to prepare a declaration of rights and "a plan of government" to maintain order and secure liberty for Virginia

---

[2] *See infra* note 18 and accompanying discussion.

[3] *See, e.g.,* New York Times Co. v. Sullivan, 376 U.S. 254, 282 (1964).

[4] Only New York and New Jersey provided no constitutional protection for the press. A good history of the press clause may be found in David A. Anderson, *The Origins of the Press Clause,* 20 UCLA L. REV. 445, 464-73 (1983). Also helpful in the preparation of this chapter were BERNARD SCHWARTZ, THE BILL OF RIGHTS: A DOCUMENTARY HISTORY, 2 vols. (1971), and A.E. DICK HOWARD, COMMENTARIES ON THE CONSTITUTION OF VIRGINIA, vol. 1 (1974).

residents.[5]   Twenty-eight members were appointed to the committee, but, ironically, two men who would become key members were not among the original twenty-eight.   James Madison, who would draft the document that would be molded into the federal Bill of Rights, was added to the committee May 16, and George Mason, who would ultimately draft the Declaration of Rights, was added May 18.

Within a month of his appointment, Mason had finished the Declaration of Rights.   It was adopted June 12, 1776, and contained this provision: "That the freedom of the press is one of the greatest bulwarks of liberty, and can never be restrained but by despotic Governments."[6]

Constitutional historian Bernard Schwartz called the document "the first true Bill of Rights in the modern American sense."[7]   The 1776 Virginia Convention was important for another reason.   As Schwartz wrote, it was

> crucial in the history of the federal Bill of Rights, both as the first constitutional instrument upon which the Federal Bill of Rights was modeled and as the training-ground of the man who was later to become known as the father of both the federal Constitution and its Bill of Rights.[8]

The father of the Bill of Rights, however, did not always favor the attachment of such a bill to the Constitution.   James Madison was originally among those Federalists who believed a

---

[5] 1 SCHWARTZ, *id.* at 231.

[6] *Id.* at 235 and 243.   North Carolina's press clause was modeled on this provision; *see id.* at 287. *See also* Anderson, *supra* note 4, at 538.

[7] *Id.* at 231.

[8] *Id.*

bill of rights to be unnecessary since the Constitution did not give the federal government the power to usurp those rights that the bill would protect.

Other Virginians disagreed. George Mason, for example, attempted without success to have the Constitutional Convention create a committee to draft a bill of rights in that hot, Philadelphia summer of 1787.[9] And during the state ratifying conventions on the Constitution, Virginia was the first of three states to propose the attachment of a federal press clause, doing so June 17, 1788.[10] Virginia's proposal, which included protection for speech as well as the press, read:

> That the people have a right to freedom of speech, and of writing and publishing their sentiments, that the freedom of the press is one of the greatest bulwarks of liberty and ought not to be violated.[11]

The support in Virginia for the inclusion of a bill of rights to the federal Constitution made an impact on Madison. Indeed, one fellow Virginian who voiced strong support for a bill of rights was James Monroe, Madison's opponent for a seat in the First Congress. Monroe made Madison's failure to call for a bill of rights a key issue in the campaign.[12] And, while Madison eventually became committed to the inclusion of a bill of rights, his first support for the bill was because he recognized that its absence made adoption of the Constitution tenuous.[13]

---

[9] *Id.* at 438.

[10] Anderson, *supra* note 4, at 471. New York and North Carolina were the other two.

[11] Va. Ratifying Convention (1788) in 2 SCHWARTZ, *supra* note 4, at 762 and 842.

[12] Anderson, *supra* note 4, at 476.

[13] *Id.* at 476-77.

Madison, therefore, struck a bargain with opponents to the Constitution: He agreed to introduce into Congress a proposed bill of rights in exchange for support for the Constitution in Virginia.[14] The bargain worked. Madison was elected to the House of Representatives; the Constitution was ratified; and, on June 18, 1788, one month after Congress opened, Madison introduced into the House a proposed bill of rights. The bill contained two amendments protecting expression:[15]

> The people shall not be deprived or abridged of their right to speak, to write, or to publish their sentiments; and the freedom of the press, as one of the great bulwarks of liberty, shall be inviolable.
> . . . .
> No state shall violate the equal rights of conscience, or the freedom of the press, or the trial by jury in criminal cases.

The second provision was included, apparently, because Madison did not believe the Bill of Rights, as part of a federal document, would automatically apply to state action.

Madison's bill was referred to a select committee, which drafted this language protecting speech and the press:

> The freedom of speech and of the press, and the right of the people peaceably to assemble and consult for their common good, and to apply to

---

[14] *See* LEONARD LEVY, EMERGENCE OF A FREE PRESS 254-55 (1985).

[15] The various versions of the speech and press clauses quoted here are published in Anderson, *supra* note 4, at 538-41.

the Government for a redress of grievances, shall not be infringed.

After debates in the House, the Bill of Rights was adopted and sent to the Senate. The Senate also adopted the bill, again altering the language of the speech and press clauses:

> That Congress shall make no law, abridging the freedom of speech, or of the press, or the right of the people peaceably to assemble and consult for their common good, and to petition the government for a redress of grievances.

It is unclear why the Senate inserted the specific reference to Congress. It may have been a simple editorial change, or it may have been a concerted effort to restrict Congress and only Congress. At any rate, a conference committee from the House and Senate eventually hammered out a final Bill of Rights. On September 25, 1789, the Speaker of the House and the Vice President signed a resolution asking President George Washington to send the twelve amendments to the governors of the states for ratification. The first two amendments were not adopted and what had been the third amendment became the first:[16]

> Congress shall make no law respecting an establishment of religion, or prohibiting the free exercise thereof; or abridging the freedom of speech or of the press, or the right of the people

---

[16] The first amendment in the original Bill of Rights related to apportionment of members of the House of Representatives, and the second amendment related to changing compensation for members of Congress.

peaceably to assemble, and to petition the Government for a redress of grievances.[17]

Amendments to the Constitution require ratification by three-fourths of the states.[18] That occurred December 15, 1791, when Virginia became the tenth of thirteen states to ratify the Bill of Rights.

Madison's proposed amendment restricting state interference with freedom of expression, of course, was not part of the Bill. Virginia adopted much of the language from that proposed amendment in its state constitution, however, where it remains today:

> That the freedom of speech and of the press are among the great bulwarks of liberty, and can never be restrained except by despotic governments; that any citizen may freely speak, write, and publish his sentiments on all subjects, being responsible for the abuse of that right; that the General Assembly shall not pass any law abridging the freedom of speech or of the press, nor the right of the people peaceably to assemble, and to petition the government for a redress of grievances.[19]

The free expression clauses of neither the Bill of Rights nor the Virginia Constitution have eliminated efforts to control speech and press, however. Within seven years of the adoption of the Bill of Rights, which specifically provided that Congress

---

[17] U.S. Const. amend. 1.

[18] U.S. Const. art. V.

[19] Va. Const. art. I, sec. 12. For a summary of the changes in the provision over the years see 1 Howard, *supra* note 4, at 251-54.

make no law abridging those freedoms, Congress passed a law doing just that.

The Sedition Act was one of a series of laws passed during the anxious early days of the Republic when the Federalists and Republicans were debating the type of government that would work best under the Constitution – a strong democracy guided by the will of the people or a conservative government with relatively strict controls.

The Sedition Act, which made it a crime to criticize the Congress or the President, was designed to silence the vituperative anti-Federalist press.[20]

Virginia responded with a series of resolutions calling for the repeal of the Act. Madison, who drafted the resolutions, argued that the federal government did not have the power to pass the restrictions and that they contradicted a free society. The Sedition Act, he wrote,

> is leveled against the right of freely examining public characters and measures and of free communication among the people thereon, which has ever been justly deemed the only effectual guardian of every other right.[21]

---

[20] The Sedition Act provided that any person who "shall write, print, utter, or publish. . . any false, scandalous and malicious writing. . . against the Government of the United States, or either house of the Congress. . . or the said President. . . or to excite against them the hatred of the good people of the United States. . . or to resist or oppose, or defeat any such law. . . shall be punished by a fine not exceeding two thousand dollars, and by imprisonment not exceeding two years," U.S. Statutes at Large I, sec. 2, at 596.

[21] James Madison, *Report of the Committee to Whom Were Referred the Communications of Various States, Relative to the Resolutions of the Last General Assembly of this State, Concerning the Alien and Sedition Laws,* in M. MYERS, ed., THE MIND OF THE FOUNDER: JAMES MADISON 243 (1981).

The Virginia Resolutions of 1798 helped establish the theory that a key purpose of the First Amendment was to provide citizens the freedom and protection to criticize their government and their governors. That theory has become a bedrock of free expression in the United States.[22]

Virginia, therefore, has possibly the strongest free expression heritage among the thirteen original states. Whether modern Virginia law remains true to that heritage, however, remains to be seen. Indeed, the Virginia Supreme Court has demonstrated a singular lack of understanding of First Amendment principles, as demonstrated by the number of free speech cases from Virginia that the U.S. Supreme Court has overturned. Those cases cover many areas of free speech jurisprudence: prior restraint,[23] post-publication punishments,[24] access to courtrooms,[25] forced oaths,[26] obscenity prosecutions,[27] defamation[28] and civil rights activities.[29]

Despite the First Amendment, therefore, and the Constitution of Virginia, which arguably offers more free speech protection than the federal document, persons who exercise their free speech rights in Virginia are often in jeopardy.

---

[22] *See, e.g.,* New York Times Co. v. Sullivan, 376 U.S. 254, 282 (1964).

[23] Bigelow v. Virginia, 421 U.S. 809 (1975).

[24] Landmark Communications, Inc. v. Virginia, 435 U.S. 829 (1978).

[25] Richmond Newspapers, Inc. v. Virginia, 448 U.S. 555 (1980).

[26] Skull v. Virginia, 359 U.S. 344 (1959).

[27] Lee Art Theatre, Inc. v. Virginia, 392 U.S. 636 (1968).

[28] Letter Carriers, AFL-CIO v. Austin, 418 U.S. 264 (1974).

[29] NAACP v. Button, 371 U.S. 415 (1963).

Mass Communication Law in Virginia

Chapter 2

VIRGINIA'S COURTS

The best way to win a lawsuit, lawyers sometimes say, is to keep it out of court. Courtrooms are unpredictable places, and one can never be sure what action a judge may take or what decision a jury may deliver.

In a judicial system, however, "uniformity of practice is regarded as a vital element,"[1] so courtrooms also possess a certain predictable nature. Protocol must be followed; there is strict adherence to procedure; rules of evidence are not violated; and, in the end, legal disputes are settled.

Those disputes are settled in Virginia much as they are in any other state: Two types of cases – criminal and civil – are adjudicated in one of two types of court – federal and state; juries determine the facts of a case, while judges and justices determine whether the law is properly applied.[2]

The system is not perfect, but it works well, and, as judges are wont to say, there is no constitutional guarantee to a perfect trial – only to a fair trial.

---

[1] VIRGINIA COURTS IN BRIEF 16 (1991). This publication is produced by the Office of the Executive Secretary, Supreme Court of Virginia.

[2] Good discussions of the court system in the United States can be found in Thomas A. Schwartz, *The Law in Modern Society,* in COMMUNICATION AND THE LAW 5-15, W. Wat Hopkins, ed. (2001); RALPH HOLSINGER and JOHN PAUL DILTS, MEDIA LAW 2-25, 4th ed. (1997); KENT R. MIDDLETON, BILL F. CHAMBERLIN and MATTHEW D. BUNKER, THE LAW OF PUBLIC COMMUNICATION 7-14, 4th ed. (1997); ROY L. MOORE, MASS COMMUNICATION LAW AND ETHICS 18-83 (1994); DON R. PEMBDER, MASS MEDIA LAW 15-31 (2001).

COURTS IN GENERAL

The mission of Virginia's court system "is to assure that disputes are resolved justly, promptly, and economically."[3] Those disputes may be between the state and an individual or between individuals.

If the state is a party to a lawsuit, the suit is generally, though not always, a criminal case. A representative of the state – called the "district attorney" or "prosecuting attorney" in some states and called the "commonwealth's attorney" in Virginia – brings an action and, if the individual is found guilty, the result may be a fine paid to the government, a jail or prison sentence or both.

In civil actions, on the other hand, the state is not a party, but acts as referee, providing the framework by which a judge and jury determine the issues in the case. A civil action is brought by one person against another when a dispute cannot be settled otherwise. Corporations and other legal entities may also be parties in lawsuits. The prevailing party in a civil action wins monetary damages, or the court may order some action to be taken, but no prison sentence is involved.

In both criminal and civil actions juries are called upon to determine the facts of the case. The jury is the sole determiner of the facts. That is, once the jury determines that certain actions occurred, that determination can be changed only under rare circumstances. On appeal, a court may determine that there were errors of law, and those errors may be of such magnitude that the jury's determination of the facts was prejudiced. If that is the case, the appellate court can order a new trial and can order that the new trial be held in accordance with its findings, but the appellate court, in most cases, cannot change the jury's determination of the facts in the case.

---

[3] VIRGINIA COURTS IN BRIEF 2.

Lawsuits are adjudicated in either state or federal courts, depending upon jurisdiction.[4] If both parties in a dispute are residents of Virginia or if there is a violation of state law or local ordinances, the dispute is settled in a state court. If one party is a resident of Virginia and the second party is a resident of some other state, however, or if there is a violation of federal law, the dispute is settled in a federal court. In addition, lawsuits claiming violation of some constitutional right are adjudicated in federal courts.

COMMONWEALTH OF VIRGINIA COURTS

Three types of trial courts exist in Virginia: circuit courts, juvenile and domestic courts and general district courts.[5]

Circuit courts are the highest trial courts in the commonwealth. One-hundred-and-twenty-two courts operate in thirty-one circuits. Circuit courts have exclusive, original jurisdiction in criminal felony cases and in all civil cases in which claims are for more than $10,000.[6] They also have appellate jurisdiction over matters heard in district courts.

---

[4] "Jurisdiction" refers to the authority of the court or the domain over which a court holds authority. Virginia courts, for example, hold jurisdiction over persons who live in Virginia.

[5] In addition to VIRGINIA COURTS IN BRIEF, *supra* note 1, THE NEWS MEDIA HANDBOOK ON VIRGINIA LAW AND COURTS (7th ed., 1986), produced by the Virginia State Bar, and GENERAL INFORMATION RELATING TO THE COURTS WITHIN EACH CIRCUIT AND DISTRICT IN VIRGINIA 1997, prepared by the Office of the Executive Secretary, Supreme Court of Virginia, were helpful in the preparation of this chapter. Virginia also maintains a web page dedicated to the state court system. Its address is http://www.courts.state.va.us/.

[6] A felony is any crime punishable by commitment to a state penitentiary. Crimes that are not felonies are called "misdemeanors;" they are punishable by no more than one year in jail, fines up to $1,000 or both.

Judges are appointed by the General Assembly for eight-year terms.

District court judges are appointed for six-year terms in each of Virginia's thirty-two judicial districts. District courts have jurisdiction in all matters where claims do not exceed $1,000 and in some matters where claims are more than $1,000 but less than $10,000. District courts also have jurisdiction in misdemeanor criminal offenses and in violations of local ordinances. In addition, special district courts have jurisdiction over matters involving juveniles and families.[7]

The judicial circuits and districts and the courts that operate within them are shown in Chart 1.

CHART 1:
JUDICIAL CIRCUITS AND DISTRICTS OF VIRGINIA

Circuit/District	Circuit Courts	District Courts
First	Chesapeake	Chesapeake
Second	Accomack Northampton Virginia Beach	Virginia Beach
2A		Accomack Northampton
Third	Portsmouth	Portsmouth
Fourth	Norfolk	Norfolk

---

[7] A juvenile in Virginia is any person aged 17 or younger.

Fifth	Isle of Wight Southampton Suffolk	Franklin City Isle of Wight Southampton Suffolk
Sixth	Brunswick Greensville Hopewell Prince George Surry Sussex	Brunswick Emporia Greensville Hopewell Prince George Surry Sussex
Seventh	Newport News	Newport News
Eighth	Hampton	Hampton

Ninth	Charles City
	Gloucester
	James City County/
	   Williamsburg
	King and Queen
	King William
	Mathews
	Middlesex
	New Kent
	Williamsburg/James City
	York
		Charles City
		Gloucester
		King & Queen
		King William
		Mathews
		Middlesex
		New Kent
		Williamsburg/James City
		   County
		York

Tenth	Appomattox Buckingham Charlotte Cumberland Halifax Lunenburg Mecklenburg Prince Edward	Appomattox Buckingham Charlotte Cumberland Halifax Lunenburg Mecklenburg Prince Edward
Eleventh	Amelia Dinwiddie Nottoway Petersburg Powhatan	Amelia Dinwiddie Nottoway Petersburg Powhatan

Twelfth	Chesterfield Colonial Heights	Chesterfield Colonial Heights
Thirteenth	Richmond	Richmond Richmond County Richmond-Manchester
Fourteenth	Henrico	Henrico
Fifteenth	Caroline Essex Fredericksburg Hanover King George Lancaster Northumberland Richmond County Spotsylvania Stafford Westmoreland	Caroline Essex Fredericksburg Hanover King George Lancaster Northumberland Spotsylvania Stafford Westmoreland
Sixteenth	Albermarle Charlottesville Culpeper Fluvanna Goochland Greene Louisa Madison Orange	Albermarle Charlottesville Culpeper Fluvanna Goochland Greene Louisa Madison Orange
Seventeenth	Arlington	Arlington Falls Church
Eighteenth	Alexandria	Alexandria
Nineteenth	Fairfax	Fairfax Vienna Division Herndon Division
Twentieth	Fauquier Loudoun Rappahannock	Fauquier Loudoun Rappahannock

Twenty-First	Henry Martinsville Patrick	Henry Martinsville Patrick
Twenty-Second	Danville Franklin Pittsylvania	Danville Franklin County Pittsylvania
Twenty-Third	Roanoke City Roanoke County Salem	Roanoke City Roanoke County Salem
Twenty-Fourth	Amherst Bedford Campbell Lynchburg Nelson	Amherst Bedford Campbell Lynchburg Nelson
Twenty-Fifth	Alleghany Augusta Bath Botetourt Buena Vista Clifton Forge Craig Highland Rockbridge Staunton Wanesboro	Alleghany Augusta Bath Botetourt Buena Vista Clifton Forge Craig Highland Lexington-Rockbridge Staunton Wanesboro
Twenty-Sixth	Clarke Frederick Page Rockingham Shenandoah Warren Winchester	Clarke Frederick/Winchester Harrisonburg/Rockingham Page Shenandoah Warren Winchester

Twenty-Seventh	Bland Carroll Floyd Giles Grayson Montgomery Pulaski Radford Wythe	Bland Carroll Floyd Galax Grayson Montgomery Pulaski Radford Wythe
Twenty-Eighth	Bristol Smyth Washington	Bristol Smyth Washington
Twenty-Ninth	Buchanan Dickenson Russell Tazewell	Buchanan Dickenson Russell Tazewell
Thirtieth	Lee Scott Wise	Lee Scott Wise/Norton Wise
Thirty-First	Prince William	Prince William

Appeals in Virginia are heard by the Virginia Court of Appeals and the Virginia Supreme Court. Only in rare cases – when the death penalty is imposed, for example – is appeal to either of these courts automatic or by right. In most cases, a petition for appeal must be made, and the court can accept or refuse the case.

Appeals in criminal, traffic and domestic cases are made to the Virginia Court of Appeals, as are appeals from decisions of administrative agencies. The decision of the court of appeals in all but criminal matters is final; decisions in criminal cases may be appealed to the Virginia Supreme Court. Appeal in most civil matters is directly to the state supreme court.

Judges to the court of appeals are appointed by the General Assembly for eight-year terms; supreme court justices are appointed for twelve years. The senior justice is the chief justice.

The justices of the state supreme court and the judges of the court of appeals are listed in Chart 2.

CHART 2:
VIRGINIA APPELLATE COURTS

Supreme Court of Virginia	Court of Appeals of Virginia
Harry L. Carrico, Chief Justice	Johanna L. Fitzpatrick, Chief Judge
Leroy R. Hassell	G. Steven Agee
Barbara Milano Keenan	Rosemarie Annunziata
Cynthia D. Kinser	James W. Benton, Jr.
Lawrence L. Koontz, Jr.	Richard S. Bray
Elizabeth B. Lacy	Rudolph Bumgardner III
Donald W. Lemons	Jean Harrison Clemente
	Larry G. Elder
	Robert P. Frank
	William Hodges, Sr.
	Robert J. Humphreys
	Jere M. H. Willis, Jr.
David B. Beach, Clerk Supreme Court of Virginia 100 N. 9th St., Fourth Floor Richmond, VA 23219 (804) 786-2251	Cynthia L. McCoy, Clerk Court of Appeals of Virginia 109 N. 8th St. Richmond, VA 23219-2305 (804) 371-8428

FEDERAL COURTS

Virginia is divided into two federal districts, each with its own trial court.

The U.S. District Court for the Eastern District of Virginia has seventeen judges who hold court in Richmond,

Norfolk and Alexandria.[8]   The U.S. District Court for the Western District has five judges who hold court in Abingdon, Charlottesville, Danville and Roanoke.   The federal district court judges and their courts are displayed in Chart 3.

In addition, the Fourth U.S. Circuit Court of Appeals is located in Richmond.   Appeals from the two district courts in Virginia, as well as from federal district courts in Maryland, North Carolina, South Carolina and West Virginia go to the Fourth Circuit.

A SAMPLE CASE

A good way to demonstrate how the court system works is to follow a typical case from the birth of a dispute through disposition.[9]

In this case, Mayor Ira Crotchity of Boondocks is suing the *Boondocks Bungler* for libel.[10]   Crotchity complains that the *Bungler* defamed him when it published an article reporting that Crotchity violated state conflict of interest laws by awarding the town's tire contract to his own Crotchity Tire Co.   The tire company was once owned by Crotchity.   Unbeknownst to the *Bungler,* however, the mayor has divested himself of any interest in the company.   Crotchity is seeking $100,000 for his damaged reputation.

---

[8] Though the judges hold court in Norfolk, their chambers – or offices – are located only in Alexandria or Richmond. *See* Chart 3.

[9] A more complete case study is in MARC FRANKLIN, THE BIOGRAPHY OF A LEGAL DISPUTE (1984).

[10] The names Mayor Ira Crotchity, Boondocks, *Boondocks Bungler,* Boondocks News Co. and Crotchity Tire Co., and the facts of this sample case are entirely fictional and are not intended to represent any person, town, newspaper, company or libel suit.

CHART 3:
U.S. DISTRICT COURTS

Eastern District of Virginia	Western District of Virginia

Alexandria
  Claude M. Hilton, Chief District
    Judge
  Leonie M. Brinkema
  James C. Cacheris (Senior Judge)
  Thomas S. Ellis III
  Gerald B. Lee
 	
Norfolk
  Robert G. Doumar (Senior Judge)
  Jerome B. Friedman
  Raymond A. Jackson
  Henry C. Morgan Jr.
  Rebecca B. Smith
 	
Richmond
  Robert E. Payne
  James R. Spencer
  Richard l. Williams (Senior Judge)
	Abingdon
	  James P. Jones
	  Glen M. Williams (Senior Judge)
	
	Danville
	  Jackson L. Kiser (Senior Judge)
	
	Charlottesville
	  James H. Michael, Jr. (Senior Judge)
	
	Lynchburg
	  Norman K. Moon
	
	Roanoke
	  James C. Turk
	  Samuel G. Wilson, Chief District Judge

Betsy Paret, District Clerk P.O. Box 21449 Alexandria, VA 22320 (703) 229-2107	Morgan E. Scott, Jr., District Clerk P.O. Box 1234 Roanoke, VA 24006 (540) 857-5100

The case is called *Crotchity v. Boondocks News Co.* The name of the party bringing the action is always first in the title of the case. In addition, legal names of individuals and companies must be used. The name of the newspaper involved may be the *Boondocks Bungler,* but the newspaper is owned by a corporation, and it is the corporation that is being sued. The party bringing the suit is the plaintiff; the party being sued is the defendant.

Crotchity's attorneys must see to it that the Boondocks News Co. is properly notified of the action. To do so, they must serve a copy of the lawsuit on an officer of the company. A copy of the suit is also placed on file in the clerk of court's office for the circuit court that holds jurisdiction. The lawsuit must specify the actions the News Company took that Crotchity believes to be improper, and it must describe how those actions were harmful to Crotchity. The case is filed in a circuit court because Crotchity is seeking more than $10,000 in damages.

Once the News Company is served, it has twenty-eight days in which to file a response. If a defendant does not respond to a lawsuit, an order will be entered finding in favor of the plaintiff. In this case, the newspaper is likely to file a *demurrer* – a statement acknowledging that the article was published, but arguing that publication of the article was not improper.

After the newspaper files its answer, the legal maneuvering will begin. Pleadings – legal arguments – will be filed; depositions will be taken; motions will be filed and argued. Depositions are statements from potential witnesses that are taken in the form of testimony outside the courtroom. Perry Mason and Ben Matlock notwithstanding, very few surprises occur in courtrooms, and there are virtually no surprise witnesses. Attorneys for both sides know what most witnesses are going to say in court long before those witnesses take the stand.

If the case is not settled before its trial date, a jury will be impaneled. Evidence will be taken, first from the plaintiff, then from the defendant. The plaintiff's evidence is designed to meet what is called a "burden of proof." The burden of proof consists of a certain number of elements – in a libel action, there are generally six (they are discussed in Chapter 4). The evidence produced by the plaintiff is designed to prove the elements in the burden of proof.

The Boondocks News Co. can win the libel action by either demonstrating that Crotchity has not proved all elements of his burden of proof or by offering a justification – or defense – for publishing the story.

After both the plaintiff and the defendant have finished presenting evidence, the judge explains the law in the case and instructs the jury as to the options it has in deciding upon a verdict. Attorneys for both sides then argue their cases to the jury. That is, the attorney for each side interprets the evidence for the jury in a light that best supports the position of that attorney's client. The jury then deliberates with a goal of reaching a verdict.

Regardless of who wins, the case is likely to be appealed. If the News Co. wins and Mayor Crotchity appeals, the name of the case will remain the same. If Mayor Crotchity wins and the News Co. appeals, however, the name of the case will change; it will become *Boondocks News Co. v. Crotchity,* because the newspaper – not Crotchity – is now bringing the action.

As previously indicated, the appeal in a civil action is to the Virginia Supreme Court, and the court may or may not accept the appeal. If the court refuses, for all practical purposes, the case is over – a case cannot leap-frog the state's highest court to the U.S. Supreme Court.

If the court accepts the case, all documents from the trial and a transcript of the trial are sent to the court. In addition, attorneys for Crotchity and the News Co. will file legal briefs – arguments describing the major points the attorneys will argue to the court and cases the attorneys say support those arguments. The court will hear oral arguments from both sides and will render an opinion.

Once again, the case will likely be appealed by the party against whom the state supreme court rules. The appeal is made to the U.S. Supreme Court by what is called a *writ of certiorari.*

And again, the Supreme Court may or may not accept the case. If the court denies *cert,* the opinion of the state supreme court stands as the final disposition. If the Supreme Court accepts *cert,* the appeal process is repeated and the Supreme Court will determine the final outcome of the case.

The procedure for a libel action filed in a federal court is similar. A case would go to federal court if there is what is called a "diversity of citizenship." If the alleged defamation about which Crotchity complained was published outside the commonwealth – in North Carolina or Maryland, for example – there would be a diversity of citizenship, and Crotchity would have filed his suit in a federal district court rather than in a state circuit court. In such a case, a federal court is required to apply the law of Virginia to the case. Appeals from federal district courts in Virginia go the Fourth U.S. Circuit Court in Richmond, then to the U.S. Supreme Court.

Chapter 3

RESTRAINTS ON EXPRESSION

Communication law is often complicated and controversial. While free expression is guaranteed by the First Amendment of the U.S. Constitution and every state constitution, the parameters of that freedom remain in dispute: What types of speech deserve protection? When is material obscene? Should broadcasters be required by law to broadcast certain types of public interest programming? How should libel law be changed to provide greater equity? When does the right of free expression outweigh other constitutionally protected rights?

Upon one point virtually all disputants agree, however: At a minimum, the free expression guarantees were designed to ensure that the government not be allowed to censor the press or the speech of individuals. Even so, courts, lawmakers and individuals often disagree on how far the prohibition against prior restraint should be taken.

The U.S. Supreme Court, for example, has said that fighting words, defamation, obscenity and speech that causes a threat to national security may be restrained.[1] The Supreme Court of Virginia has similarly noted that the guarantees of free

---

[1] *See, e.g.,* Near v. Minnesota, 283 U.S. 697 (1931); Chaplinsky v. New Hampshire, 315 U.S. 568 (1942); Roth v. U.S., 354 U.S. 476 (1957).

speech and press in the First Amendment and in the Virginia Constitution are not absolute.[2]

The question generally addressed by the courts, therefore, is not *whether* lines should be drawn prohibiting the publication of certain material, but *where* the lines should be drawn. This chapter focuses on efforts by Virginia courts to draw those lines.

Efforts to restrain speech in Virginia are not unusual. This despite the claim by the Virginia Supreme Court's that the commonwealth's constitutional protection of speech and press is more encompassing than that granted by the federal constitution.[3] Efforts to censor speech in the commonwealth, however, have generally been accompanied by bitter debate.

In April 1993, for example, the Fairfax County library board, in the face of legal threats, voted nine-to-three to keep the *Washington Blade* in its collections and in the lobbies of the system's twenty-two branch libraries. The weekly, gay-oriented newspaper had been in the library system's periodical collections since 1985, but some patrons complained in December 1992 when library officials allowed the paper to be distributed in the lobbies of branch libraries. Opponents of the newspaper threatened to sue the county for promoting sodomy, which is illegal in Virginia,[4] but the lawsuits haven't materialized. The Montgomery-Floyd Regional Library came under similar attack when residents complained that it held in

---

[2] Landmark Communications v. Commonwealth, 217 Va. 699, 703, 233 S.E.2d 120, 124 (1977).

[3] Robert v. Norfolk, 188 Va. 413, 420, 49 S.E.2d 697, 700 (1948). *See* quotation accompanying *infra* note 59. Prior restraint is defined in this chapter as any effort by the government to restrain expression, including post-expression punishment. The Virginia Supreme Court, however, does not consider post-expression punishment as a form of prior restraint. *See infra* note 20.

[4] *Virginia Library to Keep Gay Paper,* EDITOR & PUBLISHER, May 8, 1993, at 11.

its collections *Daddy's Roommate,* a children's book about the daily life of a gay father and his lover.[5]

Almost as heated was a dispute over the Confederate flag in Danville in March 1995. The Danville City Council ordered the flag removed from the city's Museum of Fine Arts and History in September 1993. The Danville Chapter of the Heritage Preservation Association, however, raised sufficient funds to erect a Civil War monument at the museum site and convinced the city council – over the votes of the council's two black members – that the Confederate flag should be flown atop the seven-foot-tall granite obelisk.[6]

A year later, threats forced an advertising company to remove a billboard that simply proclaimed "Diversity Enriches." No one had complained about the billboard on a heavily traveled road in Christiansburg until a photo appeared in a newspaper. Then, Frank Amburn of Outdoor East Advertising said, he received more than fifty calls, most complaining about the sponsors of the billboard: "Gay & Straight Citizens of Southwest Va." Some callers threatened to destroy other billboards placed by the company, so he decided to replace the message and issue a refund.[7]

Another billboard of sorts, ironically, has caused a different kind of controversy in Charlottesville. When the Thomas Jefferson Center for the Protection of Free Expression and others in the city decided to erect some type of monument to free expression, they faced opposition. The monument was to be a 7-foot by 50-foot blackboard, upon which anyone could

---

[5] Mara Lee, *Library Board Delays Decision on Book,* THE ROANOKE TIMES, March 17, 1994, at C1.

[6] Wes Allison, *Confederate Flag Waves in Danville,* THE RICHMOND TIMES-DISPATCH, March 27, 1995, at A1; Wes Allison, *Following the Flag Into Battle,* THE RICHMOND TIMES-DISPATCH, March 28, 1995, at B1.

[7] Kathy Loan, *Ad Manager: Threats Killed 'Diversity' Billboard,* THE ROANOKE TIMES, January 25, 1996, at C1.

write anything at any time. Some citizens were afraid swear words and swastikas would appear on the blackboard. Others were worried about hate speech. Eventually the blackboard was approved.[8]

These last two cases are not examples of prior restraint. The restrictions – or potential restrictions – were caused, not by the government, but by individuals. Citizens feared either who was speaking or what the speech might be rather than of the content of specific speech. The examples, however, demonstrate that, at times, society can be as inhibiting of free speech as the government. Indeed, many efforts – successful and otherwise – to restrain speech never make it to court.

When cases do make it into Virginia courts, they have focused primarily on two types of prior restraint: (a) prohibitions against publishing specific types of information, that is, content-based prohibitions, and (b) restrictions on expressive conduct.

CONTENT-BASED CENSORSHIP

Government entities in Virginia have often attempted to restrict expression on the basis of content. Most often, those efforts have been unsuccessful, but only because the U.S. Supreme Court has intervened. At least four times, beginning in the early 1970s, the U.S. Supreme Court has overturned efforts at censorship that courts in Virginia had allowed.

Prior Restraint From Richmond to Washington

In 1971 Jeffrey C. Bigelow was convicted of violating a Virginia statute making it illegal to encourage or promote the procurement of an abortion.[9] Bigelow, managing editor of the *Virginia Weekly* of Charlottesville, had published an

---

[8] *See* Ellen Goodman, *In Charlottesville, a Monument to the Right of Free Speech,* in THE ROANOKE TIMES, May 24, 2001. A19.

[9] Va. Code sec. 18.1-63 (1950).

advertisement for a New York abortion referral service. The ad noted that abortions were illegal in Virginia, but were legal in New York and were not restricted by residency requirements.[10] Bigelow argued to the Virginia Supreme Court that he was not encouraging abortions, but was merely providing information for women who had decided not to carry their pregnancies to term.[11] The court upheld his conviction, however. First, the court ruled, the language of the advertisement "constituted an active offer to perform a service, rather than a passive statement of fact."[12] Second, the court said the statute did not violate the First Amendment of the Constitution, which was designed to protect the dissemination of information or opinion rather than commercial advertising, which the government can regulate.[13]

The U.S. Supreme Court disagreed. In *Bigelow v. Virginia* the Court held that the advertisement contained information of interest to a diverse audience, and the fact that a service was being offered did not remove it from constitutional protection.[14] The Virginia statute, therefore, unconstitutionally infringed upon Bigelow's First Amendment rights.

Two years later, in *Virginia State Board of Pharmacy v. Virginia Citizens Consumer Council,*[15] the Court upheld a ruling by a three-judge panel of the Eastern District of Virginia[16] that a law prohibiting the advertisement of

---

[10] Bigelow v. Commonwealth, 213 Va. 191, 191 S.E.2d 173 (1972), *rev'd* 421 U.S. 809 (1974). At the Supreme Court level the case is titled Bigelow v. Virginia.

[11] 213 Va. at 193, 191 S.E.2d at 174.

[12] *Id.*

[13] 213 Va. at 194-95, 191 S.E.2d at 175.

[14] 421 U.S 809, 822 (1974).

[15] 425 U.S. 748 (1976).

[16] Virginia Citizens Consumer Council, Inc. v. State Board of Pharmacy, 373 F. Supp. 683 (E.D. Va. 1974).

prescription drug prices was unconstitutional. The listing of the drug prices, the Court held, was information consumers had a right to receive, and, therefore, it could not be restrained.[17]

Almost as if on schedule, in another two years the Supreme Court once again ruled against Virginia. The case began as *Landmark Communications v. Commonwealth.*[18] The *Virginian-Pilot* of Norfolk published an article about an inquiry into possible disciplinary action against a judge by the state's Judicial Inquiry and Review Commission. State law prohibits the release of any information about hearings of the commission.[19] The *Virginian-Pilot* was convicted of violating the statute and fined $500.

Landmark Communications, which owns the *Virginian-Pilot,* argued to the Virginia Supreme Court that the statute involved unconstitutional prior restraint and that the state had not overcome the heavy presumption against the statute's constitutionality. Even if the statute did not restrain the press, Landmark argued, the state had failed to prove that the publication of the confidential proceedings caused a clear and present danger to the administration of justice.[20]

The state supreme court held that the statute did not constitute prior restraint, but provided for post-publication punishment.[21] And, the court held, there was ample evidence that publication of the confidential information from the commission would constitute a clear and present danger to the orderly administration of justice.[22]

---

[17] 425 U.S. at 763-65.

[18] 217 Va. 699, 233 S.E.2d 120 (1977), *rev'd* 435 U.S. 829 (1978). At the U.S. Supreme Court level the case is titled Landmark Communications v. Virginia.

[19] Va. Code sec. 2.1-37.13 (1950).

[20] 217 Va. at 704, 233 S.E.2d at 124.

[21] *Id.*

[22] 217 Va. at 712, 233 S.E.2d at 129.

Similar arguments were used in two cases that never reached the U.S. Supreme Court. In *Leonard v. Fields*[23] the U.S. District Court for the Western District of Virginia ruled that a sheriff had not acted improperly when he fired two deputies who took employee complaints to the county's board of supervisors. Sheriff J. Trigg Fields said he considered the action of the deputies tantamount to mutiny, and the federal court ruled that the deputies were attempting to constitutionalize employee grievances by making First Amendment arguments.[24]

And, in *McBride v. Roanoke Redevelopment and Housing Authority,*[25] the same court held that the authority did not violate the free speech rights of its director by firing him for insensitive comments he made about the poor. The court held that the authority's legitimate interest in maintaining a favorable public perception outweighed the director's free speech rights. "A perception of the individual charged with overseeing the daily operations of the Authority as insensitive to the plight of the poor," the court held, "unquestionably would hinder the efficiency of the public services it provides – providing housing to low income individuals."[26]

It's unclear what would have happened if *Leonard* or *McBride* reached the U.S. Supreme Court, but in *Landmark Newspapers* the Court did not find persuasive arguments that the publication of information about the Judicial Inquiry and Review Commission would affect the efficiency of that agency. A news organization, the Court held, could not be punished for the truthful publication of information about the conduct of

---

[23] 791 F. Supp. 143 (W.D. Va. 1992).

[24] *Id.* at 144.

[25] 871 F. Supp. 885 (W.D. Va. 1994).

[26] *Id.* at 893.

public officials.[27]   The commonwealth has a right to keep the information confidential, the Court noted, but once the information is in the hands of the press, there can be no punishment for the publication of that information.[28]

The Supreme Court nipped efforts by the commonwealth to censor information for the fourth time in 1996. The Court ruled that year that the University of Virginia unconstitutionally withheld funds from an organization that published a Christian-oriented newspaper.   The university argued in *Rosenberger v. Rector and Trustees, University of Virginia*[29] that to provide the funds would violate the establishment clause of the First Amendment, but the Court held the action was content-based discrimination and, therefore, violated free-speech guarantees.

Wide Awake Productions was a student organization at the University of Virginia, but when the organization sought monies from the university's student activities funds to publish its newspaper, the funding was denied because the organization was religious. The U.S. District Court for the Western District of Virginia granted summary judgment for the university.[30] The Fourth U.S. Circuit Court of Appeals, though finding that the university's guidelines for disseminating student activities funds discriminated on the basis of content, affirmed the District Court's ruling on grounds that the discrimination was justified by the compelling state interest in maintaining strict separation between church and state.[31]

The Supreme Court disagreed. "It is axiomatic," the Court held, "that the government may not regulate speech based

---

[27] 435 U.S. at 841-42.

[28] *Id.* at 840-41.

[29] 515 U.S. 819 (1996).

[30] 795 F. Supp. 175 (W.D. Va. 1992).

[31] 18 F.3d 269, 281 (4th Cir. 1994).

on its substantive content or the message it conveys."[32] That, the Court held, is exactly what happened to Wide Awake Productions.

The U.S. District Court for the Eastern District of Virginia found that the commonwealth misapplied the establishment clause in yet another case. In *Pruitt v. Wilder*[33] the court struck down a prohibition by the Virginia Department of Motor Vehicles on references to deities on personalized license plates.

Dan F. Pruitt wanted a license plate that read "GODZGUD," but was denied that plate because of a DMV policy statement prohibiting the issuance of license plates with references to "drug culture, lewd and obscene words, deities, or combinations which might otherwise be offensive."[34] References to deities, the court held, did not violate the establishment clause of the First Amendment, and the policy was a viewpoint-based regulation of speech which violated that amendment.[35]

In addition, the Supreme Court, in effect, invalidated Virginia's "Son-of-Sam" statute in 1991 when it ruled that a similar statute from New York was unconstitutional.[36]

Son-of-Sam statutes are named for New York mass murderer David Berkowitz, who signed notes about his murders as the "Son of Sam." When news circulated that Berkowitz was attempting to sell the rights to his story to book publishers, New York passed the first Son-of-Sam statute in the country in an attempt to prohibit criminals from profiting from stories about

---

[32] 515 U.S. at 828.

[33] 840 F. Supp. 414 (E.D. Va. 1994).

[34] *Id.* at 415-16.

[35] *Id.* at 417-18.

[36] Simon & Schuster, Inc. v. New York Crime Victims Board, 502 U.S. 105 (1991).

their crimes. Ironically, Berkowitz never profited from the book publication of the accounts of his murders despite the fact that the passage of New York's Son-of-Sam statute came too late to apply to him.[37] He was prohibited from profiting by state laws already in place. Nevertheless, many states passed similar statutes.

Virginia's law provides that no person convicted of a crime or found not guilty by reason of insanity may profit from any "movie, book, newspaper, magazine, radio or television production or live entertainment or publication of any kind," if "an integral part of the work is a depiction or discussion of the defendant's crime or an impression of the defendant's thoughts, opinions, or emotions" about the crime.[38] Any money earned by such expression must go into an escrow account for five years and be used to compensate victims of the person's crimes, to pay fines or to pay legal fees. At the end of the five years, the defendant can claim twenty-five percent of the remaining funds, with seventy-five percent going to the Criminal Injuries Compensation Fund.[39]

The New York law struck down by the U.S. Supreme Court had similar provisions. The Court held, however, that the law was a content-based restriction: "It singles out income derived from expressive activity for a burden the State places on no other income, and is directed only at works with a specific content."[40] The state, the Court noted, was unable to explain why it should have any greater interest in compensating victims from the proceeds of storytelling over any of a criminal's other assets. Nor was there any justification in

---

[37] For more on Son-of-Sam statutes, see Sue S. Okuda, *Criminal Antiprofit Laws: Some Thoughts in Favor of Their Constitutionality,* 76 CALIF. L. REV. 1353 (1988).

[38] Va. Code sec. 19.2-368.20 (1950).

[39] Va. Code sec. 19.2-368.21 (1950).

[40] 502 U.S. at 116.

distinguishing between the expressive activity of a criminal and any other "fruits of crime" the criminal may have earned.[41]

Virginia's Son-of-Sam law was more narrowly drawn than that of New York. In Virginia, a person must be convicted of a crime or found not guilty by reason of insanity before falling under the provisions of the law. In New York, a person need only confess to having committed a crime – and that confession might be found only in the expressive activity.

The distinction would likely have had little bearing on the Supreme Court's opinion, however. The Court's ruling was based, not on whether the speaker was convicted of committing a crime or merely confessed to criminal activity. The Court found the statute unconstitutional because it was content-based. Virginia's statute, though more narrowly drawn, is also content-based because it regulates the subject matter of expressive activity.

Prior Restraint of Sexually Explicit Material

Sexually explicit material has been a source of controversy in many locales, and Virginia is no different. The commonwealth has made multiple efforts to restrict access to such material, some successful, some not. Courts have ruled, for example, that sexually explicit magazines can be withheld from prisoners, and that the commonwealth can restrict state employees from accessing sexually explicit Internet sites. On the other hand, a library was not allowed to install screening software on its computers, and a law prohibiting access to sexually explicit web sites was found to be unconstitutional.

The U.S. District Court for the Western District of Virginia held that sexually explicit material could be withheld from prison inmates because the material had a negative impact

---

[41] 502 U.S. at 119-20.

on security, discipline, order, public safety and rehabilitation.[42] The Fourth U.S. Circuit Court of Appeals reversed the judgment in the case on grounds that a company whose publication is restricted from prisoners must be given notice and the right to appeal, but did not address the finding that the material affected the operations of a prison.[43]

But, in a ruling that significantly limits the rights of state employees, the Fourth Circuit ruled in 1999 that the state may limit access to objectionable web sites by state employees, even if the employees need access to those sites for research purposes.[44]   In 1996, the general assembly passed a law restricting state employee access to web sites containing sexually oriented material.[45]   The law would allow access to such web sites by a state employee if access was directly related to the employee's job and if the employee received permission from a supervisor. A group of university professors, with the assistance of the American Civil Liberties Union, sued to have the act declared unconstitutional, arguing that enforcement of the law would hamper their ability to conduct research. Research interests ranged from gender roles and sexuality to Victorian poets.

The U.S. District Court for the Eastern District of Virginia held that the law was unconstitutional.[46]   The court recognized that the government, in some circumstances, could restrict the speech of employees, but also recognized that there is both an individual and societal interest in free speech activities of government employees. Those interests, the court

---

[42] Hodges v. Commonwealth, 871 F. Supp. 873, 877 (E.D. Va. 1994), *rev'd on other grounds,* Montcalm Publishing Corp. v. Beck, 80 F.3d 105 (4th Cir. 1996).

[43] *Montcalm,* 80 F.3d at 109.

[44] Urofsky v. Gilmore, 167 F.3d 191 (4th Cir. 1999).

[45] Va. Code secs. 2.1-804 - 805 (1950).

[46] Urofsky v. Allen, 995 F. Supp. 634 (E.D. Va. 1998).

said, must be balanced against the government's interest in restricting the speech.[47] When the government restrictions are based on content, the court added, the government must demonstrate a compelling interest and the restrictions must be narrowly tailored to meet that interest.[48]

The provision that access to sexually explicit material may be approved only "to the extent required in conjunction with a bona fide, agency-approved research project" makes the act even more obnoxious, the court held. The restriction allows agencies, rather than employees, to determine the types of research "required" by employees as well as the type of research that is "bona fide."[49] The court also noted that a number of content-neutral alternatives already existed to accommodate the problems about which the government is concerned.[50]

The Fourth Circuit reversed the decision. The court found significant the distinction between speech made by a person acting primarily as a citizen and speech made by a person acting primarily as a state employee. The employees were making the claim, the court held, that they were entitled to access in their capacity as state employees, so they could not simultaneously claim that the access was related to their capacity as citizens involved in speech on matters of public concern. Therefore, since the regulation limited the speech of state employees in their capacity as employees and since the state had the right to retain the ability to control the manner in which its employees discharge their duties, the regulation was constitutional.[51]

---

[47] *Id.* at 636.

[48] *Id.* at 637.

[49] *Id.* at 641-42.

[50] *Id.* at 643.

[51] 167 F.3d at 196.

In yet another cyberspace case, a policy by which the Loudoun County Library installed software on its computers intended to block web sites containing child pornography or obscene material was held by the federal district court for the Eastern District of Virginia to be unconstitutional.[52] Applying the strict scrutiny test, the court found that protecting patrons from sexual harassment was a compelling government interest, but that the policy was not narrowly tailored to meet that interest.[53] The court also found the policy to be infirm because it was devoid of standards by which a reviewing authority could determine if the blocking decisions were appropriate.[54]

The federal district court for the Western District of Virginia also had problems with a law restricting Internet use. The court issued a preliminary injunction in August 2000, prohibiting the enforcement of a state law prohibiting the distribution of to juveniles of sexual material that is harmful to them.[55] The law, the court held, was not narrowly tailored and infringed on First Amendment rights.[56] The preliminary injunction means the law cannot be enforced until a lawsuit challenging the statute's constitutionality is decided.

Miscellaneous Restrictions

Not all restrictions on expression are designed to inhibit the dissemination of information and ideas. Indeed, some restrictions are designed to promote an understanding of issues important to the public. Virginia law contains several restrictions that fall into this category. For example, state law

---

[52] Mainstream Loudoun v. Board of Trustees of the Loudoun County Library, 24 F. Supp. 2d 552 (E.D. Va. 1998).

[53] *Id.* at 565-67.

[54] *Id.* at 569.

[55] PSINET v. Chapman, 108 F. Supp. 2d 611 (W.D. Va. 2000).

[56] *Id.* at 624.

makes it illegal for a person to knowingly give a news organization false information for the purpose of publication or broadcast;[57] and any person from attaching to a newspaper any communication that was not authorized by the publisher.[58]

RESTRICTIONS ON EXPRESSIVE CONDUCT

A variety of types of types of expressive conduct – from selling magazine subscriptions, to marching, to burning crosses and flags – have come under attack in Virginia. Most efforts at suppression, however, have been ruled unconstitutional.

Even the state supreme court, which, as has been demonstrated, is not known for granting broad protection to expression, has been hesitant in restricting expressive conduct. The court, for example, noted that "The Constitution of Virginia is broader than that of the United States in providing that 'any citizen may freely speak, write and publish his sentiments on all subjects.'"[59]   And the court defined "publishing" as bringing information before the public for sale or distribution.[60]

In addition, the court has ruled that "the streets and highways belong to the public."   Since they are "natural and proper places for the dissemination of information and opinion by citizens," they cannot be regulated in a manner that restricts free expression.[61]   An ordinance prohibiting the door-to-door solicitation of magazine subscriptions without a license, therefore, was held to be unconstitutional.

---

[57] Va. Code sec. 18.2-209 (1950).

[58] Va. Code sec. 18.2-210 (1950).

[59] Robert v. Norfolk, 188 Va. 413, 420, 49 S.E.2d 697, 700 (1948).

[60] Id.

[61] 188 Va. at 419, 49 S.E.2d at 700.

Similarly, the court has held that citizens have a right to march, parade or demonstrate on public streets.[62] Towns and cities may impose reasonable time, place and manner restrictions and may require parade permits, but those permits may not be arbitrarily refused and may not be refused based upon the nature or content of the demonstration. And potential marchers may not be required to meet unreasonable criteria before being granted the permits.[63]

Courts are generally more willing to protect private property from individuals or groups making free speech arguments. The Virginia Supreme Court held, for example, that the state constitution does not allow a person to distribute information on private property once that person is ordered to stay off the property.[64] By statute, Virginia also prohibits the picketing of a private residence, unless certain requirements are met.[65] And, the Fourth U.S. Circuit Court of Appeals has held that the Freedom to Access to Clinic Entrances Act of 1994, which prohibits protestors from obstructing access to abortion clinics, is constitutional.[66] The act, the court held, does not prohibit protesting, the distribution of handbills and other forms of expression, so long as the activities are carried out in a non-violent, non-obstructive manner and physical obstruction or threat of force is not used to interfere with a person's right to enter the clinics.[67]

The state supreme court has also held that noise ordinances are unconstitutional if they are aimed at restraining

---

[62] York v. Danville, 207 Va. 665, 669, 152 S.E.2d 259, 263 (1967).

[63] 207 Va. at 670, 152 S.E.2d at 263-64.

[64] Hall v. Commonwealth, 188 Va. 72, 49 S.E.2d 369 (1948).

[65] Va. Code sec. 18.2-419 (1950). Picketing of a labor dispute, construction site or a place wherein a meeting on a topic of general public interest is occurring are allowed, even if private dwelling places are involved.

[66] American Life League, Inc. v. Reno, 47 F.3d 642 (4th Cir. 1995).

[67] *Id.* at 648.

controversial speech which, by its nature, may upset the peace and tranquility of the community.[68] The government may restrain efforts to incite riots or the participation in riots, but may not restrain speech simply because it may cause unrest due to its uncomfortable or obnoxious nature.[69]

The court also ruled that Virginia's unlawful assembly ordinance is unconstitutionally overbroad.[70] The case began when demonstrators in Charlottesville were arrested after refusing to disperse as ordered by law enforcement officers. The court held that the statute, in addition to punishing genuine disturbances of the peace, would punish peaceful gatherings for purposes protected by the First Amendment. The ordinance, therefore, was unconstitutional, and a conviction for its violation could not stand.[71]

Virginia's law prohibiting mutilation of the flag is probably unconstitutional as well, though there has been no ruling on the statute. In 1989 the U.S. Supreme Court struck down as unconstitutional the Texas flag-desecration law, which was very similar to Virginia's.[72]

Virginia, in fact, has two statutes aimed at protecting the U.S. and Virginia flags. One statute prohibits flying a flag that has been altered in any way,[73] while a second states that "No person shall publicly burn with contempt, mutilate, deface,

---

[68] Thomas v. Danville, 207 Va. 656, 663, 152 S.E.2d 265, 270 (1967).

[69] Id.

[70] Owens v. Commonwealth, Ferguson v. Commonwealth, 211 Va. 633, 179 S.E.2d 477 (1971). The unlawful assembly statute, Va. Code sec. 18.1-254.1 (1950), was repealed in 1975.

[71] 211 Va. at 637, 197 S.E.2d at 481.

[72] Texas v. Johnson, 491 U.S. 397 (1989).

[73] Va. Code sec. 18.2-487 (1950).

defile, trample upon, or wear with intent to defile any such flag, standard, color, ensign or shield."[74]

The U.S. Supreme Court held in the Texas case that burning a flag as a sign of dissatisfaction with governmental policies was protected political speech. A year later, the Court reiterated that point in striking down the newly adopted Flag Protection Act.[75] Since Virginia's law is aimed at the suppression of speech, it is probably unconstitutional as well.

Virginia legislators have recognized that some forms of expressive conduct are designed to frighten or intimidate people and have taken steps to prohibit those acts. Three statutes, in particular, are designed to prohibit the use of recognized symbols for purposes of intimidation.

Virginia law prohibits the burning of a cross on private property, "with the intent of intimidating any person or group of persons."[76] The U.S. Supreme Court struck down a cross-burning ordinance from St. Paul, Minn., in 1992, but Virginia's ordinance may survive constitutional scrutiny.[77] The St. Paul ordinance made it illegal to burn a cross with intent to intimidate any person on the basis of the person's race, creed or religion. The Court held that the act was discriminatory because it singled out certain groups for protection from intimidating speech and did not protect all groups.[78] Virginia's law, on the other hand, protects from intimidation by cross burning, any person or group.

A conviction under the statute is nevertheless being challenged before the Virginia Supreme Court. Barry Black

---

[74] Va. Code sec. 18.2-488 (1950).

[75] U.S. v. Eichmann, 496 U.S. 310 (1990).

[76] Va. Code sec. 18.2-423 (1950).

[77] R.A.V. v. St. Paul, Minn., 505 U.S. 377 (1992). *See, e.g., Terry: Va. Law Made to Survive Court Challenge,* ROANOKE TIMES & WORLD-NEWS, 23 June 1992, A2.

[78] 505 U.S. at 391-92.

organized and led a Ku Klux Klan rally on private property in Cana, Va., August 22, 1998, at which a cross was burned. Black was eventually convicted of violating the cross-burning law and was fined $2,500.[79] The conviction was affirmed by the Virginia Court of Appeals in a one-sentence opinion: "For the reasons stated in *O'Mara v. Commonwealth*. . . we affirm the judgment of the trial court." This, even though the facts of the *O'Mara* case were significantly different from those of *Black v. Commonwealth*.[80]

Attorneys for Black are arguing to the Virginia Supreme Court that the statute engages in viewpoint discrimination and, therefore, is unconstitutional. The case is significant because it will force the state high court to address an issue at the heart of First Amendment protections: Whether the government can silence certain kinds of speech because the government finds that speech obnoxious. When this book went to press, the state court had not ruled in the case.

Virginia's swastika law, however, is not as broad as the cross-burning statute. The law prohibits the placing of a swastika in order to intimidate any person or group, but only prohibits the placement of the swastika on a place of worship or on an educational facility or community center owned by a religious body.[81] The law has not been challenged, but the swastika law, like the St. Paul cross-burning statute, is aimed a protecting a particular class of people – those who are members of organized religions.

Similarly, a federal court has upheld as constitutional Virginia's ordinance prohibiting an adult from wearing a mask

---

[79] Black v. Commonwealth, Petition for Appeal, 2-7.

[80] *Id.* at 7. *See also,* O'Mara v. Commonwealth, 33 Va. App. 525, 535 S.E.2d 175 (2000).

[81] Va. Code sec. 18.2-433.1 (1950).

except in certain circumstances.[82] The court held that a mask worn as part of Ku Klux Klan egalia did not convey a particularized message apart from the remainder of the costume and contributed nothing to the message already conveyed, so First Amendment rights were not infringed.[83]

ABUSIVE LANGUAGE

At times, abusive language can almost take on the role of conduct. If language is aimed at an individual, for example, and is so offensive that it is likely to cause the individual to respond with physical violence, the language falls into that category of speech the U.S. Supreme Court has called "fighting words" and is not protected.[84]

Virginia law prohibits fighting words and certain other classes of abusive language from being uttered in both face-to-face contexts and over the airwaves. Both statutes have been held to be constitutional by Virginia courts, but for different reasons.

Virginia prohibits a person from cursing or abusing another person with language "reasonably calculated to provoke a breach of the peace."[85] The statute has been held to apply only to fighting words, that is, words that would have a direct tendency to cause acts of violence;[86] if remarks are not made in a face-to-face confrontation, the statute does not apply. The Virginia Court of Appeals, therefore, held that abusive language

---

[82] Va. Code sec. 18.2-422 (1950). A mask can be worn as part of a holiday costume, as part of a person's professional attire, as part of a theatrical production or for medical reasons.

[83] Hernandez v. Superintendent, Fredericksburg-Rappahonnock Joint Security Center, 800 F. Supp. 1344, 1351 (E.D. Va. 1992).

[84] Chaplinsky v. New Hampshire, 315 U.S. 568 (1942).

[85] Va. Code sec. 18.2-416 (1950).

[86] Mercer v. Winston, 214 Va. 281, 199 S.E.2d 724 (1973), *cert. denied,* 416 U.S. 988 (1974).

made in an argument between two neighbors was not actionable because the neighbors were separated by at least fifty-five feet and a chain-link fence.[87]

Under that rationale, the same court should also find that the Virginia statute prohibiting the use of profane, threatening or indecent language over the public airwaves, including telephone lines, is unconstitutional.[88] After all, there can be no face-to-face confrontation in such circumstances. The court, however, found just the opposite. The legislature intended for the law to address harassing conduct, the court found, and ruled that, as applied, "it proscribes conduct and not speech."[89] Similarly, the Virginia Court of Appeals has held that repeatedly making threatening phone calls by telephone was a form of stalking, that is, was conduct rather than speech.[90]

---

[87] Hershfield v. Commonwealth, 14 Va. App. 381, 417 S.E.2d 876 (1992).

[88] Va. Code sec. 18.2-427 (1950).

[89] Perkins v. Commonwealth, 12 Va. App. 7, 14, 402 S.E.2d 229, 233 (1991).

[90] Parker v. Commonwealth, 24 Va. App. 681, 485 S.E.2d 150 (1998), *cert. denied* 523 U.S. 1071 (1998).

Mass Communication Law in Virginia

Chapter 4

LIBEL

In Old Virginia, an insult could prompt fisticuffs or, worse yet, a pistol duel. Violent responses to verbal insults became so common, in fact, that in 1810 the Virginia General Assembly adopted what has become known as "the insulting words statute," specifically to force disputes from the streets into courtrooms.[1]

The effort worked. Dueling was reduced, but battles in the courtroom, in their own way, were no easier settled than they had been in the streets. Libel cases in Virginia, like everywhere else, are difficult to resolve. Complex burdens of proof require extensive preparation and hours of complicated deposition taking and evidence presentation. Both plaintiffs and defendants face grueling tasks.

Before turning to an examination of how libel law works, however, some background on libel in Virginia is necessary.

---

[1] Va. Code sec. 8.01-45 at 55 (1950). The Virginia Supreme Court noted in 1887 that the purpose of the statute was to suppress "the barbarous custom of dueling," Chaffin v. Lynch, 83 Va. 106, 112, 1 S.E. 803, 806 (1887). A good brief history of libel law in Virginia is in David C. Kohler, *Toward a Modern Defamation Law in Virginia: Questions Answered, Questions Raised*, 21 RICH. L. REV. 3, 41-44 (Fall 1986). Also helpful in the preparation of this chapter was Alexander Wellford and Craig T. Merritt, *Survey of Virginia Defamation Law*, LIBEL DEFENSE RESOURCE CENTER 50-STATE SURVEY 1999-2000.

THE DEVELOPMENT OF LIBEL LAW IN VIRGINIA

The insulting words statute and Virginia common law have spawned lawsuits that fall into three distinct classes: insulting words, libel and slander. Early in the history of libel law, lawsuits could be filed when words were written or spoken that "from their usual construction and common acceptance are construed as insults and tend to violence and breach of the peace."[2] Depending upon the circumstances of the case, a lawsuit might have fallen into any of the three categories. The causes of action were similar in many ways, but there were some important differences.

Libel involved written words that, like slander or insulting words, might cause a breach of the peace. The cause of action was not related to whether a person was actually injured, but was based on insult, embarrassment or hurt feelings. Since injured feelings existed regardless of whether a published charge was true or false, truth was no defense. A requirement for a successful libel action was that the insulting words be published to some third party, that is, to someone other than the author and the subject of the alleged defamation.

Similarly, since an insult involved words – spoken or written – specifically intended to harm an individual, truth was no defense in an insulting words case. Unlike libel, however, whether a third person heard or read the words was irrelevant; it was only necessary for the person at whom the words were aimed to hear them.

The third type of legal action in Virginia's defamation history was slander, which involved spoken words that caused specific monetary loss. The sole basis for a slander suit was whether a person had suffered some pecuniary loss that could be documented. Like libel, publication to a third party was necessary for the suit to be actionable.

---

[2] Va. Code sec. 8.01-45 (1950).

As Virginia's libel law evolved, the three causes of action were merged. Virginia courts no longer recognize a distinction between an action for libel and an action for slander,[3] and have established that the only distinction between an action for libel and one for insulting words is that publication to a third party is necessary for a successful libel action.[4] In fact, under modern Virginia law, an action for insulting words cannot exist absent a libel case unless the words may also be construed as fighting words.[5]

Libel, which is the focus of this chapter, may also be brought under Virginia common law.[6] Libel occurs when words are published in some written form that tend to injure the reputation of a person or to render that person odious, contemptible or ridiculous.[7]

Libel law is not that simple, however. Modern libel law recognizes that some forms of defamation are justified. It is defamatory, for example, to report that a mayor is accepting bribes for assuring that certain businesses receive contracts with his city. The report would certainly injure the mayor's reputation and would render him contemptible. If the report is true, however, or is published after it was thoroughly investigated, the publisher of such a report is not likely to lose a libel action.

---

[3] *See, e.g.,* Fleming v. Moore, 221 Va. 884, 889, 275 S.E.2d 632, 635 (1981), *citing* Shupe v. Roses' Stores, 213 Va. 374, 376, 192 S.E.2d 766, 767 (1972).

[4] Davis v. Heflin, 130 Va. 169, 173-74, 107 S.E. 673, 675 (1921); Hines v. Gravins, 136 Va. 313, 319, 112 S.E. 869, 870 (1923), *cert. denied*, 265 U.S. 583 (1923).

[5] Dwyer v. Smith, 867 F.2d 194, 195-96 (4th Cir. 1989). For more about fighting words, *see* Chapter 3.

[6] *Shupe*, 213 Va. at 376, 192 S.E.2d at 767.

[7] *Chaffin,* 83 Va. at 113, 1 S.E. at 807.

Responsible news organizations, therefore, cannot fulfill their role in society without publishing defamations. But only unjustified defamations are punishable. The responsibility for proving that punishment is warranted lies with the plaintiff.

THE LIBEL PLAINTIFF

To win a libel action in Virginia, a plaintiff must prove that there was publication of a false, actionable statement about the plaintiff, to some third person, that tended to injure the plaintiff's reputation.[8] The plaintiff must also prove that there was some degree of fault on the part of the defendant.[9] In simplest terms, then, a libel plaintiff's burden of proof consists of publication, identification, defamation, falsity, damages and fault.

Publication

The defendant in a libel action is not necessarily the author of defamatory material; libel law is generally unconcerned with authors. The person who faces liability is the publisher – that person who makes the defamatory material available to some third party. A person may – with complete immunity – write anything about anyone. In addition, an author may show the defamatory material to the person about whom it is written without fear of liability.[10] If the author shows the material to anyone else, however, the material has been

---

[8] *Michie's Jurisprudence,* Libel & Slander sec. 12.

[9] Gazette, Inc. v. Harris, 229 Va. 1, 325 S.E.2d 713 (1985); *Fleming,* 221 Va. 884, 275 S.E.2d 632 (1981).

[10] While no libel action would be successful under the circumstances described here, at one time Virginia law would have allowed an action for insulting words. *See* discussion accompanying *supra* notes 1-2.

published and a lawsuit is possible.[11]   The author is not being sued for creating the defamation, but for publishing it.

Publication is probably the easiest element for a libel plaintiff to prove, particularly in cases involving the media. While plaintiffs in non-media libel actions may lose their cases because they could not show that the defamatory material had been published,[12] publication is almost never at issue in cases involving mass communication.   The plaintiff only needs to show that the questionable material appeared in some published form – a newspaper, magazine, book, brochure, poster, film or broadcast, for example.   It is not necessary to prove that someone actually saw the allegedly defamatory material; if it appeared in a mass medium, the presumption is that it was published.   This last point is particularly noteworthy in cases involving the posting of material on an Internet web page.

Since the publisher, rather than the author, is the target of a libel action, however, newspapers and magazines can be sued for publishing material produced by non-employees: by free-lance writers, by news and feature syndicates, by advertisers and even by readers.[13]

In addition, each time a defamation is published, the republication is considered a new libel, and the publisher of the new libel may be sued.   In some cases – if the republication "is

---

[11] *See, e.g., Davis,* 130 Va. 169, 107 S.E. 673 (1921), in which the mailing of a letter to a third person was ruled to be publication. The one exception to the rule is sharing the allegedly defamatory material with someone who has a duty related to the incidents described in the publication. *See, e.g.,* Cobb v. Rector and Visitors of the University of Virginia, 84 F. Supp. 2d 740, 750 (W.D. Va. 2000).

[12] *See, e.g., Dwyer,* 867 F.2d at 195, and Food Lion, Inc. v. Melton, 250 Va. 144, 450-51, 485 S.E.2d 580, 584-85 (1995).

[13] *See, e.g.,* Story v. Norfolk-Portsmouth Newspapers, Inc., 202 Va. 588, 118 S.E.2d 668 (1961), in which the *Virginian-Pilot* was sued for material published in a letter to the editor.

the natural and probable consequence" of the original publication – the original publisher can also be sued for the republication.[14] In one 1989 Virginia case, for example, the Fourth U.S. Circuit Court of Appeals held that a publisher of financial information was responsible for a defamatory article published by the *Roanoke Times & World-News* because the article was based on a report issued by the company.[15]

Identification

In legal parlance, "identification" means that the defamatory material is "of and concerning" the plaintiff. The plaintiff is required to prove that the defamation specifically identified him or her.[16]

Identification is usually easy to prove. When a person is named, that person has been identified. There are other methods of identification, however. Someone may be identified by use of a photograph or cartoon, for example. And, of course, identification can be based entirely upon description. That has happened in at least two Virginia cases – one from the Virginia Supreme Court and one from the federal court for the Eastern District of Virginia.[17]

Port Packet Corp. v. Lewis was one of four cases the Virginia Supreme Court resolved under the title *Gazette, Inc. v.*

---

[14] Weaver v. Beneficial Finance Co., 199 Va. 196, 199, 98 S.E.2d 687, 690 (1957).

[15] Blue Ridge Bank v. Veribanc, Inc., 866 F.2d 681, 689-90 (4th Cir. 1989).

[16] In March 200, the Virginia Supreme Court refused to allow a law suit to proceed when the plaintiff in the case wanted to remain anonymous. America Online v. Anonymous Publicly Traded Company, ___ Va. ___, 542 S.E.2d 377 (2001)

[17] Federal courts play a limited role in libel actions; they are required to rule in accordance with state law or, in the absence of precedent, to rule as they determine state courts would.

Harris.[18]   The case involved two articles and an editorial on child abuse published by the *Alexandria Port Packet* in July 1980. In one article, the newspaper identified with the fictional name of "Mark" a nine-month-old boy who died in an Alexandria hospital. "Mark" died of severe head injuries two days after being admitted to the hospital. The article reported that police believed "Mark" to be the victim of "a vicious attack." "Mark's" parents were not named in the article, and a last name for the child was not used.[19]

The newspaper was sued by E. Grey Lewis and Carolyn G. Lewis, who argued that they had been identified as abusive parents. Though not named, they said the many similarities between "Mark" and their own son, Edward, would cause readers to believe the Lewises were responsible for their son's death.[20]

The Virginia Supreme Court agreed. Like "Mark," Edward was nine months old and had severe head injuries. Edward was admitted to the same hospital as "Mark" was in the hospital the same length of time before dying and died at about the same time as "Mark." In addition, the court found to be significant the newspaper's stated intent to identify abusive parents. The jury could have concluded, therefore, that the newspaper intended to refer directly to "Mark's" abusers and, in so doing, had identified the Lewises as abusive parents.[21] This

---

[18] 229 Va. 1, 325 S.E.2d 713 (1985). In addition to the *Gazette* case, 229 Va. at 20, 325 S.E.2d at 728, and *Port Packet,* 229 Va. at 32, 325 S.E.2d at 735, the cases settled in the opinion were Charlottesville Newspapers, Inc. v. Matthews, 229 Va. at 27, 325 S.E.2d at 732 and Fleming v. Moore, 229 Va. at 43, 325 S.E.2d at 742. This was the second time *Fleming* reached the Virginia Supreme Court. *See* text accompanying *infra* notes 40-41.

[19] 229 Va. at 33, 325 S.E.2d at 736.

[20] 229 Va. at 32-33, 325 S.E.2d at 735-36.

[21] 229 Va. at 37-38, 325 S.E.2d at 738-39.

was so, the court said, even though neither the reporter who wrote the article nor his editors knew the true identities of "Mark" or his parents.[22]

In some cases, description need not be nearly so specific for a court to rule that a plaintiff was identified. A single reference to a "live-in lover" in a satirical song broadcast by a radio station was sufficient for identification in the case of *Freedlander v. Edens Broadcasting, Inc.,* out of the Eastern District of Virginia.[23]

Eric M. Freedlander and Donna Leigh Keeler sued WRVQ for broadcasting a song they said defamed them. Freedlander, a well-known Richmond businessman, was identified by name, but Ms. Keeler was not. She brought suit alleging that the station identified her by a reference to Freedlander's live-in lover. The court agreed,[24] noting that Ms. Keeler had been referred to in news articles as Freedlander's roommate and companion.[25]

Virginia law also recognizes that members of groups can be identified, even if not named, if the groups are relatively small. If a group is very large, however, individuals may not bring libel actions because the size of the group precludes the identification of individual members. It has been difficult to pinpoint the threshold that allows identification, but it generally lies between twenty-five and one hundred.[26]

---

[22] 229 Va. at 39, 325 S.E.2d at 739.

[23] 734 F. Supp. 221 (E.D. Va. 1990).

[24] *Id.* at 224.

[25] *Id.* at 227, note 11.

[26] Good discussions of group libel are Kyu Ho Youm, *Libel: The Plaintiff's Case* in COMMUNICATION LAW WRITERS GROUP, COMMUNICATION AND THE LAW, W. Wat Hopkins, ed. 93-94 (2001); KENT R. MIDDLETON, BILL F. CHAMBERLIN and MATTHEW D. BUNKER, THE LAW OF PUBLIC COMMUNICATION 4th ed. 95-96 (1997); ROY L. MOORE, MASS COMMUNICATION LAW AND ETHICS 286-88 (1994).

Virginia cases give little guidance in determining the cutoff in the commonwealth. There have been no appellate cases since 1924, when the state supreme court ruled that a member of the House of Delegates was not identified in a publication that criticized, but did not name, one member of the general assembly. The court held:

> If the class or group is a very large one, and there is little or nothing which applies to the particular person who brings the action, his right of recovery will generally be denied. . . . On the other hand, if the language employed is directed towards a comparatively small or restricted group of persons, then any member thereof may sue.[27]

While there have been no appellate cases involving group libel since 1924, there have been at least a couple of circuit court cases. In 1989, a Fairfax County circuit court judge held that a lawsuit brought by a foreign-educated physician could not be maintained when the defamed group was "foreign medical graduates." The group, the court held, consisted of more than 120,000 doctors and more than 20 percent of all doctors licensed and practicing in the United States.[28] And, in February 2001, a circuit court dismissed a libel suit brought by a police officer in Elkton against the town and the town's mayor.[29] In this second case, the court held that the U.S. Supreme Court case of *New York Times Co. v. Sullivan*

---

[27] Ewell v. Boutwell, 138 Va. 402, 409, 121 S.E. 912, 914 (1924).

[28] Shah v. Medical Economics Co., 17 Va. Cir. 162 (No. 88984, Fairfax Circuit, May 17, 1989).

[29] Dean v. Town of Elkton, 2001 WL 184223 (No. CL00-11958, Rockingham Circuit, Feb. 21, 2001).

barred lawsuits against the government or a government agency, no matter what the size of the agency.[30]   The U.S. Supreme Court noted in *Times v. Sullivan,* the circuit court held, that the constitution does not allow government officials to assume they have been identified by impersonal attacks on the government and respond with libel actions.[31]

Virginia cases related to the issue of identification are limited, but *Port Packet* and *Freedlander,* in particular, seem to indicate that courts in the commonwealth are likely to give a libel plaintiff the benefit of the doubt. If courts determine that a reasonable person might be able to identify an individual from references in a defamatory publication, the courts are likely to rule that identification has been proved.

Defamation

Libel plaintiffs, in order to win their cases, must prove that published material tends to lower their reputations or cause them harm. The words themselves, taken in "their plain and natural meaning," must be harmful.[32]   If they are, the defamation is called libel *per se* – libel on its face. If the published words do not constitute libel *per se,* a libel plaintiff can only win by showing special damages, that is, by documenting exactly how much money has been lost as a result of the libel.[33]

Virginia also recognizes libel *per quod.* Libel *per quod* occurs when published words are not defamatory on their face, but become defamatory when additional, unpublished facts are

---

[30] *Id.* at 4-5.

[31] *Id.* at 4, quoting *Times v. Sullivan,* 376 U.S. 254, 291-92 (1964).

[32] *Carwile,* 196 Va. at 7, 82 S.E.2d at 591-92.

[33] *Shupe,* 213 Va. at 376, 192 S.E.2d at 767.

taken into account.[34]   Special damages must also be proved in a case of libel *per quod.*

In Virginia, published material is libelous *per se* if:[35]

(1) it charges an individual with some criminal offense involving moral turpitude for which the person could be indicted and punished;

(2) it charges an individual with having some contagious disease that would exclude the person from society;

(3) it charges an individual with being unfit to perform the duties of the person's job or with an absence of integrity needed to perform those duties;

(4) it damages a person's ability to earn a living.

Only words that fit into one of these four categories are libelous *per se* and can be the basis of a lawsuit without proof of special damages.   It is not libelous *per se* in Virginia to report that someone is insane, for example, since a charge of insanity does not fall into one of the four categories, even though such a report is likely to injure a person's reputation and even though many states would recognize such a report to be defamatory.   For such a charge to be actionable in Virginia, there must be a showing of special damages.[36]

Similarly, a false report that a person is dead does not fall into one of the four categories and, therefore, is not libelous *per se.*[37]   And, in a heated union dispute, the words "cocksucker" and "motherfucker" did not convey a false representation of any illegal acts, so they were not

---

[34] A good discussion of libel *per quod* is in Wilder v. Johnson Publishing Co., 551 F. Supp. 622, 623-625 (E.D. Va. 1982).

[35] *Carwile,* 196 Va. at 7, 82 S.E.2d at 591;   M. Rosenberg & Sons v. Craft, 182 Va. 512, 518, 29 S.E.2d 375, 378 (1944).

[36] *M. Rosenberg,* 182 Va. at 518, 29 S.E.2d at 378;   Mills v. Kingsport Times-News, 475 F. Supp. 1005, 1008-09 (W.D. Va. 1979).

[37] O'Neil v. Edmonds, 157 F. Supp. 649, 651 (E.D. Va. 1958)

defamatory.[38] But a report that an attorney is unethical is likely to directly affect the attorney's profession, so the charge is libelous *per se*.[39]

The Virginia Supreme Court's strict adherence to the four categories of libel *per se* can be seen in a 1981 case involving a charge that a white professor at the University of Virginia was a racist. While racism might be an offensive charge, it is neither a contagious disease nor a criminal offense, the court held, so it was not libelous *per se*. In addition, the court originally held that there was no showing that the charge injured the professor's ability to earn a living; the fact that it "might have" affected the plaintiff's work was insufficient.[40] During the second trial of the case, however, the professor was able to introduce evidence that, on appeal, satisfied the court that a charge of racism would materially affect his relations with his students and the atmosphere in his classroom, so the charge was held to be defamatory.[41]

Despite the apparently clear language used to specify the types of words that are defamatory *per se,* some definitional problems have arisen. The first of the four categories, for example, seems to imply that virtually any charge that a person has committed a criminal offense is defamatory. The Virginia Supreme Court, however, has apparently adopted the rule that for such a charge to be actionable, the crime must be serious – a felony, "punishable by imprisonment in a state or federal

---

[38] Crawford v. United Steel Workers, AFL-CIO, 230 Va. 217, 234, 335 S.E.2d 828, 839-39 (1985).

[39] *Carwile,* 196 Va. at 8, 82 S.E.2d at 592.

[40] *Fleming,* 221 Va. at 891, 275 S.E.2d at 636. This case returned to the state supreme court as part of *Gazette,* 229 Va. at 43, 325 S.E.2d at 742.

[41] *Gazette (Fleming),* 229 Va. at 47, 325 S.E.2d at 744.

institution" – or it must be "regarded by public opinion as involving moral turpitude."[42]

Charges that a person is guilty of a misdemeanor, therefore, are not actionable unless the misdemeanor involves moral turpitude, which the court defined as, "'an act of baseness, vileness, or depravity in the private and social duties which a man owes to his fellow man, or to society in general, contrary to the accepted and customary rule of right and duty between man and man.'"[43] Under that construction, the court held that a charge of "commercial bribery" in business, while not punishable by imprisonment, was an offense involving moral turpitude and, as such, was defamatory *per se.*[44]

The state supreme court, during the same year, also found that identifying a woman as being unmarried and pregnant resulted in a charge that the woman had committed the crime of fornication and was defamatory *per se. Charlottesville Newspapers, Inc. v. Matthews* was one of the four cases the court resolved in its *Gazette* opinion. Debra C. Matthews, who was married and pregnant, brought suit because she was repeatedly identified in a news story as "Miss Matthews." She was a key witness in the trial of a man she said raped her. The man was found not guilty of rape but guilty of fornication, which is the voluntary sexual intercourse by an unmarried person and is a misdemeanor in Virginia.[45]

The court held that someone reading the story could have believed that Mrs. Matthews was also guilty of fornication

---

[42] Great Coastal Express, Inc. v. Ellington, 230 Va. 142, 147, 334 S.E.2d 846, 850 (1985).

[43] *Great Coastal Express,* 230 Va. at 147, 334 S.E.2d at 850, *quoting* Tasker v. Commonwealth, 202 Va. 1019, 1024, 121 S.E.2d 459, 463 (1961).

[44] 230 Va. at 147, 334 S.E.2d at 850.

[45] *Gazette (Charlottesville Newspapers),* 229 Va. at 27-28, 325 S.E.2d at 732-33.

and became pregnant as a result.[46]   What the court failed to recognize, apparently, was that, had the newspaper reported the courtesy title correctly, the reader could have presumed that Mrs. Matthews was guilty of adultery, which would have been no less defamatory.[47]

Ironically, a federal district court in Virginia ruled five years later that the crime of fornication did not involve moral turpitude, within the definition adopted by the Virginia Supreme Court, and, therefore, was not defamatory.[48]   In *Freedlander,* which involved a woman who was identified as a "live-in lover," the court ruled that cohabitation and fornication might have once involved moral turpitude, but no longer. "This is evidenced," the court held, "by the absence of prosecutorial vigor." There have been no arrests for such behavior, the court noted, and the crimes were established to inhibit prostitution.[49]

In addition, the same district court has held that it is not defamatory *per se* to report that someone is in bankruptcy and is subject to criminal investigation, because neither of these charges suggests the commission of an offense punishable by imprisonment.[50]

Indeed, it has been difficult for courts to settle on exactly what a crime involving moral turpitude is. Lying on legal documents, for example, is a crime involving moral turpitude,[51] but concealing liquor on which taxes have not been

---

[46] 229 Va. at 29, 325 S.E.2d at 733.

[47] *See* Kohler, *supra* note 1, at 29.

[48] *Freedlander,* 734 F. Supp. at 226.   *See* discussion of this case accompanying *supra* notes 23-25.

[49] *Id.* at 226.

[50] *Id.* at 225.

[51] Chesapeake and Ohio Railway Company v. Hanes, 196 Va. 806, 813, 86 S.E.2d 122, 126 (1955).

paid,[52] operating a lottery and gambling house[53] and drunkenness[54] are not crimes involving moral turpitude.

Other examples of defamatory statements are:

- that a jewelry salesman is a shark;[55] or that a salesman is inefficient and provides unsatisfactory service;[56]
- a charge of shoplifting;[57]
- a charge that a corporation or its personnel pose a serious security risk;[58]
- a charge that a black politician's failure to support a second black politician harmed the black community.[59]

Some examples of non-defamatory statements are:

- a charge that someone is discourteous;[60]
- a statement that checks should not be accepted from an individual;[61]
- a statement that an individual was terminated from his position because his job performance was unsatisfactory.[62]

---

[52] Burford v. Commonwealth, 179 Va. 752, 765, 20 S.E.2d 509, 514 (1942).

[53] Parr v. Commonwealth, 198 Va. 721, 725, 96 S.E.2d 160, 164 (1957).

[54] Pike v. Eubank, 197 Va. 692, 699, 90 S.E.2d 821, 827 (1956).

[55] Powell v. Young, 151 Va. 985, 994, 144 S.E. 624, 626 (1928).

[56] Montgomery Ward v. Nance, 165 Va. 363, 377, 182 S.E. 264, 269 (1935), but see *infra* note 62.

[57] Zayre of Virginia, Inc. v. Gowdy, 207 Va. 47, 49, 147 S.E.2d 710, 713 (1966); *Food Lion,* 250 Va. at 151, 458 S.E.2d at 585.

[58] Swengler v. ITT Corporation Electro-Optical Products Division, 933 F.2d 1063, 1071 (4th Cir. 1993).

[59] *Wilder,* 551 F. Supp. at 625.

[60] Auvil v. Times-Journal Co., 10 Media L. Rep. (BNA) 2302, 2303 (E.D. Va. 1984).

[61] *Shupe,* 213 Va. at 375, 192 S.E.2d at 767.

[62] McBride v. Roanoke Redevelopment and Housing Authority, 871 F. Supp. 885, 891-92 (W.D. Va. 1994), but see *supra* note 56.

Virginia law specifies that, for words to be considered defamatory, they "are to be taken in their natural sense, and as they would naturally be understood by those reading [the] publication."[63] This does not mean, however, that the defamation must always be explicit. As the state supreme court has held:

> . . . it is not necessary that the defamatory charge be in direct terms but it may be made indirectly, and it matters not how artful or disguised the modes in which the meaning is concealed if it is in fact defamatory. Accordingly, a defamatory charge may be made by inference, implication or insinuation.[64]

But, the court added, "the meaning of the alleged defamatory language cannot, by innuendo, be extended beyond its ordinary and common acceptation."[65] Questions therefore, are not defamatory if the context of those questions indicates that several answers exist, since inquiry, however embarrassing or unpleasant to its subject, is not defamatory. If the questions, however, may be read as assertions of fact, they may be defamatory. The language must be read so as to "make that certain which is in fact uncertain."[66]

---

[63] *Ewell,* 138 Va. at 416, 121 S.E. at 916.

[64] *Carwile,* 196 Va. at 7, 82 S.E.2d at 592. *See also Zayre,* 207 Va. at 50, 147 S.E. at 713.

[65] 196 Va. at 7, 82 S.E.2d at 592.

[66] Chapin v. Knight-Ridder, Inc., 993 F.2d 1087, 1094 (4th Cir. 1993).

Falsity

Falsity is a key element in a libel action, since only false statements are actionable. To publish that the mayor accepts bribes, as previously indicated, will certainly damage the mayor's reputation, but a news organization cannot be required to pay damages for publishing the statement if it is true. Similarly, a commentator cannot be required to pay damages for stating his or her opinion that the mayor has done a poor job while in office. Since opinions are neither true nor false, in Virginia they are not actionable. Opinion is discussed in detail later in this chapter.

The Virginia Supreme Court has held that a plaintiff in a libel action is required to prove that the published, defamatory material is false.[67] That is, the court made a clear distinction between defamation and falsity. Words may be defamatory, the court held, but unless those same words are false, there can be no libel action.[68] In addition, the material shown to be false must be at the heart of the libel claim. It is insufficient for the plaintiff to prove that there were some slight inaccuracies in a long publication since "slight inaccuracies of expression are immaterial. . . ."[69] Similarly, a federal court held in a Virginia case that, "a plaintiff cannot combine the damaging nature of certain true statements with the falsity of other, immaterial statements in order to provide the basis for a defamation claim."[70] In addition, the issue turns on the truth of what was published. For example, the truth of a published report about a person being arrested and charged with a crime focuses on

---

[67] *Gazette,* 229 Va. at 15, 325 S.E.2d at 724-25.

[68] Shenandoah Publishing House, Inc. v. Gunter, 245 Va. 320, 326, 427 S.E.2d 370, 372 (1993).

[69] Saleeby v. Free Press, Inc., 197 Va. 761, 763, 91 S.E.2d 405, 407 (1956). *See also,* James v. Haymes, 163 Va. 873, 884, 178 S.E. 18, 22 (1935).

[70] Chapin v. Greve, 787 F. Supp. 557, 563 (E.D. Va. 1992).

whether the individual was, in fact, arrested and charged, not on the individual's ultimate guilt or innocence.[71]

Finally, language that is merely rhetorical hyperbole, the Virginia Supreme Court has held, cannot be proved to be false and, therefore, cannot be the basis of a libel action. Attorneys for Sharon Yeagle, an administrator at Virginia Tech, argued to the court in 1998 that a line published in the *Collegiate Times,* the university's student newspaper, identifying her as "Director of Butt Licking," charged Ms. Yeagle with the crime of sodomy. The identification line was part of a computer template used in layout that editors failed to change during the production of the paper.[72]

Montgomery Circuit Court Judge Ray Grubb dismissed the lawsuit, finding that the phrase was "void of any literal meaning" and that no reasonable person would have believed the line to convey any factual information about Yeagle.[73] The state supreme court affirmed the ruling, holding that "speech which does not contain a provably false factual connotation, or statements which cannot reasonably be interpreted as stating actual facts about a person cannot form the basis of a common law defamation action."[74] The court noted that the identification line is "disgusting, offensive and in extremely bad taste," but, "it cannot reasonably be understood as stating an actual fact about Yeagle's job title or her conduct, or that she committed a crime of moral turpitude."[75]

---

[71] Pilkenton v. Kingsport Publishing Corp., 270 F. Supp. 315, 317 (W.D. Va. 1967), *aff'd* 395 F.2d 989 (4th Cir. 1967).

[72] Yeagle v. Collegiate Times, 255 Va. 293, 497 S.E.2d 136, 137 (1998).

[73] 255 Va. at 295, 497 S.E.2d at 137.

[74] *Id.*

[75] 255 Va. at 297, 497 S.E. 2d at 138.

Damages

Without proof that a defamatory publication caused actual injury, a plaintiff cannot win a defamation action.[76] The type of injury a plaintiff suffers is represented by three types of damages, the award of each being determined by a jury.

- *Actual* or *compensatory damages* are damages paid to a plaintiff for injury caused by libel *per se*. The damages are to compensate for an injured reputation and the accompanying embarrassment, humiliation, emotional suffering and physical suffering. Evidence must generally be introduced demonstrating the injury. That evidence can be testimony about the negative effects the publication had on the subject of the publication. The testimony may demonstrate a personality change in the subject that the subject felt humiliation and embarrassment or that the subject feared that the attitude of neighbors and friends might change.[77] If the lawsuit is based on libel *per se* and the material is not of public concern, however, compensatory damages are presumed if the plaintiff can demonstrate the existence of negligence.[78] Negligence is discussed in detail later in this chapter.

- *Special damages* are those for which the libel plaintiff can show specific pecuniary loss.[79] They represent out-of-

---

[76] Landmark Communications, Inc. v. Macione, 230 Va. 137, 334 S.E.2d 587 (1988).

[77] *See, e.g.,* Richmond Newspapers, Inc. v. Lipscomb, 234 Va. 277, 299, 362 S.E.2d 32, 45 (1987); *Gazette,* 229 Va. at 25, 40-42 and 47-50, 325 S.E.2d at 731, 740-41 and 744-45.

[78] *Great Coastal Express,* 230 Va. at 151, 334 S.E.2d at 852.

[79] The Virginia Supreme Court has caused some confusion over how special damages are to be defined and awarded, but the distinction between compensatory and special damages delineated here seems to be holding true, at least for the present. *See* Kohler, *supra* note 1, at 40-41.

pocket loss and must be documented. In cases of libel *per se,* special damages may be paid in addition to compensatory damages. In other defamation actions, a showing of special damages is required for any award.

- *Punitive damages* are awarded a plaintiff specifically to punish the publisher of a defamation for particularly reprehensible conduct. Punitive damages may not be awarded without proof of actual malice on the part of the publisher, regardless of whether the published material is of public concern.[80] Actual malice is discussed in detail later in this chapter. In Virginia, the award of punitive damages has been limited to $350,000.[81] On the surface, the limitation seems significant. Traditionally, punitive damages are considerably higher than compensatory or special damages, so a limitation on punitive damages adds a degree of protection for the press. Attorneys can always find ways to circumvent the letter of the law, however. When Tony Morrison, a former student and football player at Virginia Tech, sued the *Collegiate Times* for defamation, for example, he sought only $350,000 in punitive damages, but sought $5 million in compensatory damages and an additional $5 million in special damages, even though he was a student at the time and could apparently demonstrate no actual loss of income.[82]

---

[80] *Great Coastal Express,* 230 Va. at 151, 334 S.E.2d at 852.

[81] Va. Code sec. 8.01-38.1 (1950).

[82] Morrison v. Collegiate Times, No. 760 CL 96 B02902-00 (Richmond Circuit, Filed Nov. 27, 1996).

Fault

The U.S. Supreme Court held in 1974 that a defamatory publication must be made with some degree of culpability on the part of the publisher before damages can be awarded.[83] The ruling, in theory, established a wide gamut of the types of fault libel plaintiffs could be required to prove in order to win their cases.

In Virginia, as in most states, however, only two types of fault have been established. Public officials and public figures are required to prove actual malice before they can win their libel actions. Private persons, on the other hand, need only prove negligence in order to win compensatory damages, but, as previously indicated, must prove actual malice if they are to win punitive damages.

Several terms, therefore, need definition: public official, public figure, actual malice and negligence.

Public officials. In *Richmond Newspapers, Inc. v. Lipscomb,*[84] the Virginia Supreme Court outlined the criteria it will use to determine whether a person is a public official. Vernelle M. Lipscomb, the head of the English Department at Thomas Jefferson High School in Richmond, sued the *Richmond Times-Dispatch* for an article about students and their parents who were dissatisfied with her teaching and classroom organization. The court noted that some state courts had ruled that public school teachers were public officials,[85] but found Lipscomb to be a private person. In so doing, the court indicated five considerations that need to be addressed in determining whether a plaintiff is a public official:

---

[83] Gertz v. Robert Welch, Inc., 418 U.S. 323, 347-48 (1974).

[84] 234 Va. 277, 362 S.E.2d 32 (1987).

[85] 234 Va. at 286, 362 S.E.2d at 36, note 3.

(1) Is the plaintiff paid with public funds? Lipscomb, as a public school teacher, was paid with public funds, but the court said other criteria were more significant.[86]

(2) Did the plaintiff have ready access to effective means of communication? The court found that Lipscomb had limited access to the media and would have difficulty, therefore, publicly rebutting the published false statements.[87]

(3) Is the plaintiff elected to office? Lipscomb was not.[88]

(4) Is the plaintiff in a policy-making position? The court found that Lipscomb did not influence or appear to influence any public affairs or school policy.[89]

(5) Is there an independent interest in the person who holds the plaintiff's position? The court found that the public had no independent interest in Lipscomb's qualifications and performance beyond a general interest in the qualifications and performance of all teachers.[90]

In a case three years earlier, the federal court for the Eastern District of Virginia held that a receptionist in an Army pediatrics center was a public official.[91] The receptionist, the court held, was the single person empowered to make appointments for the clinic. In addition, her position required her to be "in constant contact with the public, including many persons who have reason to be fearful and distressed." Her performance in her position, therefore, "is clearly a matter of

---

[86] 234 Va. at 284-87, 362 S.E.2d at 35-37.

[87] 234 Va. at 284-85, 362 S.E.2d at 35-36.

[88] 234 Va. at 285-86, 362 S.E.2d at 36-37.

[89] 234 Va. at 286, 362 S.E.2d at 37.

[90] 234 Va. at 286-87, 362 S.E.2d at 37.

[91] *Auvil,* 10 Media L. Rep. (BNA) at 2304.

public concern, and accordingly, she should be treated as a public official."[92]

While it is difficult to guess what types of people may be classified as public officials by courts in Virginia, one can presume that any person elected to office will be so classified, as will almost any person in government whose position invites public scrutiny. Public figures are equally tricky to classify.

Public Figures. Three types of public figures have been identified in Virginia cases: public figures for all purposes, also called general purpose public figures; public figures for limited purposes, or vortex public figures; and involuntary public figures. The most common, by far, are all purpose and limited-purpose public figures.

An all-purpose public figure is a person who occupies a position of persuasive power and influence[93] or who has widespread fame or notoriety.[94] Achievement of general-purpose public-figure status is a significant feat. Neither community involvement nor newsworthiness is synonymous with public figure status. As one federal court held in a Virginia case, "The attainment of general public figure status is not to be lightly assumed, even if the plaintiff is involved in community affairs, and requires clear evidence of such stature."[95]

A limited-purpose public figure need not have achieved the widespread fame of an all-purpose public figure. Indeed, a person must meet specific requirements in order to become a

---

[92] 10 Media L. Rep. (BNA) at 2304.

[93] *Fleming,* 221 Va. at 891, 275 S.E.2d at 637.

[94] *Freedlander,* 734 F. Supp. at 229, *citing Gertz,* 418 U.S. at 351.

[95] *Blue Ridge Bank,* 866 F.2d at 687.

public figure for limited purposes. Generally, those requirements are that:[96]

   (1) there be an ongoing public controversy;

   (2) the person voluntarily entered the controversy; and

   (3) the person attempted to affect the outcome of the controversy.

Some courts, including the Fourth U.S. Circuit Court of Appeals in a Virginia case, have added two requirements:[97]

   (4) the person has access to channels of effective communication; and

   (5) the person's public figure status was retained at the time of the defamation.

Because of the limited role of federal courts in state libel law, for the ruling of the Fourth U.S. Circuit Court of Appeals to be incorporated into state law, it must be adopted by the state supreme court.[98]

The same court has also broadly interpreted the requirement that there be an ongoing public controversy, holding that the controversy could be caused by the plaintiff. In *National Foundation for Cancer Research, Inc. v. Council for Better Business Bureaus, Inc.,* the court held that, "Even though the 'public controversy' which formed the basis of this lawsuit arose almost entirely from the Foundation's solicitation and use of funds for its cancer research, the mere fact that the NFCR generated the controversy does not preclude a finding that there was, in fact, a controversy."[99] The rationale for this broad interpretation of the rule is that a person who voluntarily

---

[96] *Gertz,* 418 U.S. at 351.

[97] Fitzgerald v. Penthouse International, Ltd., 691 F.2d 666, 668 (4th Cir. 1982).

[98] *See supra* note 17.

[99] 705 F.2d 98, 101 (4th Cir. 1983). *See also Freedlander,* 734 F. Supp. at 230.

engages in a course of action that invites attention and comment is a public figure.[100]

The Foundation, the court held, "vigorously sought the public's attention" with a massive solicitation effort of almost sixty-eight million pieces of mail over three years, in which it declared its objective to make its name a household word and "extolled its judicious use of donated funds."[101] Therefore, it invited comment over its use of funds, creating a controversy, particularly since the campaign led to many inquiries of Better Business Bureaus about the Foundation.[102]

Similarly, the Fourth U.S. Circuit Court of Appeals found a scientist involved in a controversy over carcinogens to be a public figure. Melvin Reuber was employed at the Frederick Cancer Research Center, which held a contract with the National Cancer Institute. Reuber disagreed with the center on whether certain pesticides were carcinogens and reported his independent research on stationary from both the center and the institute. When he was reprimanded for his activity, a report of the reprimand was leaked to an industry newspaper. Reuber sued for libel and argued that he was a private person.[103]

The court held that (a) Reuber had significant access to channels of effective communication; (b) he voluntarily assumed a role of special prominence, (c) in order to affect the outcome of the controversy; (d) that the controversy existed prior to the publication of the defamatory statements; and, (e) that Reuber retained public figure status at the time of the

---

[100] *Freedlander,* 734 F. Supp. at 230.

[101] *National Foundation,* 705 F.2d at 101.

[102] *Id.* at 101.

[103] Reuber v. Food Chemical News, Inc., 925 F.2d 703, 706-07 (4th Cir. 1991)(en banc), *cert. denied,* 501 U.S. 1212 (1991).

publication.[104] The case was from a federal court in Maryland, but the Fourth Circuit Court would likely apply the same test to libel cases from other states within its jurisdiction.

In other Virginia cases, a bank was held to be neither a public figure for general purposes nor for limited purposes because it had "no widespread power or persuasive influence" and because the controversy into which it was drawn was not of the bank's making;[105] a company hired by a county water authority was held to be neither a general-purpose nor limited-purpose public figure;[106] a chimney manufacturer whose product was disparaged in a magazine article was held to be a private person;[107] and a college professor was held to be a private person.[108]

The college professor was determined to be a private person even though he became involved in a controversy surrounding a proposed housing project near his home and spoke in opposition to the project at public hearings.[109] Similarly, the grandparents of a child involved in a prolonged and highly publicized child custody dispute, who were referred to as "abusers" and who held regular press conferences, were determined to be private persons because they did not voluntarily assume a role of especial prominence.[110]

While the most common public figures are all-purpose of limited-purpose, the U.S. Supreme Court, in *Gertz,* indicated

---

[104] 925 F.2d at 708-10.

[105] *Blue Ridge Bank,* 866 F.2d at 687-88.

[106] Arctic Co. v. Loudoun Times-Mirror, 624 F.2d 518, 521 (4th Cir. 1980), *cert. denied,* 449 U.S. 1102 (1982).

[107] General Products Co. v. Meredith Corp., 526 F. Supp. 546, 551-52 (E.D. Va. 1981).

[108] *Fleming,* 221 Va. at 891-92, 275 S.E.2d at 637.

[109] 221 Va. at 891-92, 275 S.E.2d at 637.

[110] Foretich v. Capital Cities/ABC, Inc., 37 F.3d 1541, 1543 (4th Cir. 1994).

that there might be a third category of public figures: involuntary public figures. The Court noted, however, that such public figures would be "exceedingly rare."[111]   And, indeed, they have been. Involuntary public figures have been discussed in only one case from Virginia. The Fourth U.S. Circuit Court of Appeals, in a 1999 case involving controversial Watergate figure G. Gordon Liddy, established a test for determining when a libel plaintiff is an involuntary public figure, but held that the person who brought a libel action against Liddy was a private person.[112]   For a libel plaintiff to be an involuntary public figure, the court held, the defendant must show that[113]

- the plaintiff had become a central figure in a significant public controversy, that the allegedly defamatory statement had arisen in the course of discussion about the public matter, and that the plaintiff was the regular focus of media reports;
- the plaintiff assumed the risk of publicity, even if not seeking to publicize views on the controversy; that is, that the plaintiff took some action or failed to act when action was required in circumstances in which a reasonable person would understand that publicity would likely inhere;
- the controversy existed prior to the publication of the defamatory statement;
- the plaintiff retained public figure status at the time of the defamation.

The court held that Ida Maxwell Wells, a secretary for the Democratic National Committee during the time of the Watergate break-in, was not an involuntary public figure. In a speech he gave at James Madison University, Liddy

---

[111] *Gertaz,* 418 U.S. at 345.

[112] Wells v. Liddy, 186 F.3d 505 (4th Cir. 1999).

[113] *Id.* at 539-40.

hypothesized that one reason for the break-in might have been to uncover information linking the finance of White House counsel John Dean to a supposed prostitution ring in which Wells was involved.[114] Wells was not a central figure in media reports on Watergate, the court held. Even in books promoting the call-girl theory, the court noted, Wells was not mentioned as a prominent player.[115]

Negligence and Actual Malice. As previously indicated, public officials and public figures – both limited-purpose and general-purpose – must prove actual malice in order to win their libel actions. Actual malice was defined by the U.S. Supreme Court as knowledge of falsity or reckless disregard for the truth.[116] It is a substantial burden of proof, requiring libel plaintiffs to prove either that the defendant was lying when he or she published the defamatory material, or that the defendant was so patently reckless that the defendant obviously did not care whether the published material was true or false.[117]

Negligence has been defined in a variety of ways,[118] and the Virginia Supreme Court has not been clear in how it defines the term. In general, the state court has defined negligence as "that degree of care which an ordinarily prudent person would exercise under the same or similar circumstances to avoid injury to another."[119]

---

[114] *Id.* at 512.

[115] *Id.* at 540-41.

[116] New York Times Co. v. Sullivan, 376 U.S. 254, 279-80 (1964).

[117] *See, e.g.,* W. WAT HOPKINS, ACTUAL MALICE 115-152 (1989).

[118] *See, e.g.,* W. WAT HOPKINS, *Negligence Ten Years After Gertz v. Welch,* JOURNALISM MONOGRAPHS (No. 93, August 1985), at 5-16.

[119] Griffin v. Shively, 227 Va. 317, 321, 315 S.E.2d 210, 212-13 (1984), *quoting* Perlin v. Chappell, 198 Va. 861, 864, 96 S.E.2d 805, 808 (1957). These were non-libel cases, but the state supreme court has applied the

The definition is common to a number of states, but some states have interpreted negligence more broadly in media cases, indicating that an ordinarily prudent person under the same or similar circumstances would necessarily be a journalist confronted with similar problems. The definition of negligence in those states, therefore, is related to the degree of care that an ordinarily prudent journalist would exercise in similar circumstances.[120] This is an important distinction since actions by a reasonably prudent journalist and a reasonably prudent person may not be identical.

The Virginia Supreme Court has made several references to the "reasonably prudent" editor or journalist.[121] Indeed, in *Richmond Newspapers, Inc. v. Lipscomb,* the court specifically referred to the type of action that would be taken by "a reasonably prudent news reporter."[122]

At the same time, however, the court has demonstrated a lack of understanding of the unique character of the newsroom. In a number of cases from other states, expert witnesses have been called to testify as to actions by journalists that might or might not be reasonable. Though not ruling outright that expert witnesses would not be allowed in Virginia courts, the state supreme court – again in *Richmond Newspapers* – upheld a ruling by a trial judge denying a defendant in a libel case the right to call expert witnesses.[123]   Expert witnesses are not needed, the court held, "concerning matters of common knowledge or matters as to which the jury are [sic] as

---

definition – or a close representation – in libel cases. *See, e.g.,* discussion accompanying *infra* notes 121-24 and 128-44.

[120] *See, e.g.,* HOPKINS, ACTUAL MALICE, *supra* note 117, at 8-13.

[121] *See, e.g., Gazette,* 229 Va. at 23, 29, 325 S.E. at 729, 733.

[122] 234 Va. at 289, 362 S.E.2d at 38.

[123] 234 Va. at 295-96, 362 S.E.2d at 42.

competent to form an opinion as the witnesses."[124] The court did not explain how members of a jury would be knowledgeable about the operation of a newsroom or the duties and expectations of reporters.

Whatever the definition of negligence in Virginia, the court has established that the rule will only apply when the material in question "makes substantial danger to reputation apparent."[125] When the material is not obviously defamatory, actual malice must be proved in order to recover damages. Therefore, the court held, "The mere negligent error or careless misstatement of fact which, on its face, does not appear to be defamatory will not result in liability."[126]

On its face, the rule seems to be an added bit of protection for the press. It does not always operate that way, however, because of the way the court has applied negligence. Indeed, one attorney knowledgeable about libel law has said the application of negligence in Virginia is likely to be highly unpredictable because of the lack of precision given the term by the court.[127]

Possibly the best way to demonstrate negligence and actual malice is to examine Virginia cases in which these fault elements were delineated.

The court's first examination of negligence came in the 1985 case of *Gazette, Inc. v. Harris*. As previously indicated, the case involved four libel suits combined by the court and settled under one title. In three of the cases, the court found evidence of negligence, and in one case the court found evidence of actual malice.

---

[124] 234 Va. at 296, 362 S.E.2d at 42.

[125] *Gazette,* 229 Va. at 15, 325 S.E.2d at 725.

[126] *Gazette,* 229 Va. at 16, 325 S.E.2d at 725-26.

[127] Kohler, *supra* note 1, at 28.

The court's most detailed examination of negligence came in the first of the four cases. A Goochland County paper, the *Gazette,* had published, as part of its regular roundup of criminal court activity, the following item:

> Harold F. Payne, aggravated sexual battery, Barbara H. Sweeny, property bond; aggravated sexual battery, James and Virginia Harris, property bond charges certified to circuit court (charges filed in the adult division of juvenile court).[128]

In fact, Payne had been charged with two counts of aggravated sexual battery; Sweeny and the Harrises were the complainants, that is, they were bringing the charges against Payne. They filed suit against the *Gazette,* claiming that the item identified them as having been charged with the crimes.

An editor at the *Gazette* testified that he believed the item to be accurate because it was a verbatim copy of a court record. To complicate matters, until the report was published, the *Gazette* had not been in the practice of including in its "Criminal Cases" column the names of complainants; previously only the persons charged had been named. The newspaper's failure to explain the significance of the names, the court held, was carelessness.[129] A jury could reasonably find, therefore, that the newspaper acted negligently in violating its long-standing custom of only publishing the names of suspects without using a format that accurately informed readers of the significance of the names.[130]

---

[128] 229 Va. at 21, 325 S.E.2d at 728.

[129] 229 Va. at 24, 325 S.E.2d at 730.

[130] 229 Va. at 25, 325 S.E.2d at 731.

But this was only part of the evidence of negligence. In affirming verdicts for Sweeny and the Harrises, the Virginia Supreme Court also found it significant that neither the reporter nor his editor sought verification for the information. That was important, the court said, because the reporter did not fully understand the documents he was examining: "The jury was entitled to conclude that the reporter was negligent because of his ignorance."[131]

In addition, evidence indicated that the only part of the court document the reporter understood was the abbreviation "CMPLNT," for "complainant." Yet, the reporter failed to identify Sweeny and the Harrises as the complainants, "an act of omission that the jury also could determine constituted negligence."[132]

In neither of the other two *Gazette* opinion cases involving negligence was the court so exacting in its examination of the facts. In *Charlottesville Newspapers, Inc. v. Matthews,* which has been discussed previously, the court found *The Daily Progress* negligent when it identified a married woman as pregnant and unmarried.

Once again, the report was written by a reporter who was inexperienced in covering courts. He based his report on a transcript of a preliminary hearing in the case, rather than attending the trial or using a transcript of the trial, and he did not talk to anyone involved in the case. In addition, he testified that the use of "Miss" rather than "Mrs." to identify the plaintiff was, "Just a slip of my memory," and the city editor testified that it never occurred to him that calling a woman "Miss" and identifying her as pregnant would be defamatory. Because of

---

[131] 229 Va. at 24, 325 S.E.2d at 730.

[132] *Id.*

all this, the court held, "evidence of the newspaper's negligence was abundant."[133]

The final negligence case in the *Gazette* opinion has also been discussed previously. E. Gray and Carolyn G. Lewis sued the *Alexandria Port Packet* claiming they were identified as abusive parents because circumstances surrounding the death of an unidentified child in an article published by the newspaper were similar to those of their own child. The article quoted Alexandria Police Sergeant Ronald Uhrig as saying the child died as a result of a vicious attack, that the child was the victim of a beating and that the police were treating the child's death as a murder. At trial, however, Uhrig testified that he never made those comments and that he had complained to the reporter about being misquoted.[134]

In addition, the reporter sought no verification of the information he received for the story because he mistakenly believed Uhrig to be in charge of the investigation into the child's death.[135]

While this was evidence of negligence, the court held, there was no evidence of actual malice; there was no evidence that the reporter or his editor knew the defamatory material was false, and "the articles were researched in depth. . ." and were "edited in a deliberate fashion with consideration given to accuracy."[136]

Research also became an issue in determining the existence of negligence and actual malice two years later when

---

[133] *Gazette (Charlottesville Newspapers),* 229 Va. at 30, 325 S.E.2d at 734. *See* discussion of the case at *supra* notes 45-47.

[134] *Gazette (Port Packet),* 229 Va. at 34-35, 325 S.E.2d at 736-37. *See* discussion of the case at *supra* notes 17-21.

[135] 229 Va. at 36, 325 S.E.2d at 737.

[136] 229 Va. at 42, 325 S.E.2d at 741.

the court decided *Richmond Newspapers, Inc. v. Lipscomb.*[137] Vernelle Lipscomb was a high school English teacher who was harshly criticized by some of her students and their parents in an article written by *Richmond Times-Dispatch* reporter Charles E. Cox. The article was initiated when a parent contacted Cox about problems students were having with Lipscomb. The reporter wrote the story after talking with at least three parents, at least three students, several of Lipscomb's colleagues, Lipscomb's principal and other administrators. Lipscomb was contacted several times by the reporter but refused to comment.[138]

The state supreme court, however, found the newspaper negligent primarily because Cox did not interview students friendly to Lipscomb. Though recognizing that the story contained information favorable to the teacher,[139] and that Cox repeatedly attempted to interview Lipscomb and her superiors to learn their side of the controversy,[140] the court found ample evidence of negligence.[141]

There was insufficient evidence of actual malice, however. Lipscomb made six claims to support her charge that the newspaper published the story with actual malice, but the court rejected all six:[142]

(1) Lipscomb claimed that the ill will of the reporter's sources raised obvious doubts as to their veracity, but the court found the only bias was due to their dissatisfaction with Lipscomb as a teacher, and there was nothing to impeach their credibility.

---

[137] *See* discussion of this case at *supra* notes 84-90.

[138] 234 Va. at 282-83, 362 S.E.2d at 34-35.

[139] 234 Va. at 292-93, 362 S.E.2d at 40.

[140] 234 Va. at 294-95, 362 S.E.2d at 41.

[141] 234 Va. at 289, 362 S.E.2d at 38.

[142] 234 Va. at 289-95, 362 S.E.2d at 38-42.

(2) Lipscomb claimed Cox was predisposed against her, but evidence to support the charge was insufficient.

(3) Lipscomb claimed that Cox resolved ambiguities against her and omitted favorable information, but the court held that, while some favorable information may have been omitted, the story contained positive, as well as negative, information.

(4) Lipscomb claimed that the newspaper should have been held to a high degree of accountability because of the absence of deadline pressure. The court noted that in each case she cited to support her argument, however, there was evidence of other reckless conduct absent from the *Richmond Newspapers* case.

(5) The court rejected Lipscomb's claim that the newspaper's decision to wait and publish the story when Cox returned to the office from a vacation was evidence of serious doubts as to the truth of the story. The fact that the newspaper wanted to double check some of the information was hardly evidence of serious doubts, the court held.

(6) There was no evidence to support Lipscomb's claim that Cox threatened her or her principal. "On the contrary," the court held, "the evidence shows that Cox was trying to persuade them to give Lipscomb's side of the controversy."[143]

What is remarkable about the *Richmond Newspapers* case is that, based on these findings, the court was able to find evidence of even negligence. The court recognized that Cox's witnesses were unimpeachable, that he had repeatedly attempted to interview Lipscomb and her superiors, and that he included favorable information about her in the story. Yet, because the court decided Cox did not interview enough sources from a specific category, the court found the newspaper

---

[143] 234 Va. at 294, 362 S.E.2d at 41.

negligent. The Virginia Supreme Court was taking on a role that the U.S. Supreme Court has specifically eschewed – the role of editor.[144]

Two other cases demonstrate the state supreme court's low threshold for fault in libel cases. In *Newspaper Publishing Corp. v. Burke* the court held that a newspaper article may have been published with actual malice when a journalist attributed controversial statements to a source who denied making the statements.[145] An aggravating circumstance was the fact that the journalist promised the source an opportunity to check the story before publication, but failed to keep the promise, even in light of a second source doubting the accuracy of the information.[146]

And, in *Fleming v. Moore* – the last of the cases settled in *Gazette* – the court held that a real estate developer "abandoned all judgment and reason" in making comments about a university professor during a controversy over a housing development.[147] The developer placed an advertisement in the student newspaper at the University of Virginia, in which he called the professor a racist, said he was being supported on the public dole at the expense of the "working people" and said the professor's stated grounds for opposing the development were a sham to conceal his effort to oppress blacks. The court held that the developer placed the ad, with insufficient evidence, to intimidate the professor in order

---

[144] *See, e.g.,* Miami Herald v. Tornillo, 418 U.S. 241, 285 (1974) and 418 U.S. at 261 (White, J., concurring); Nebraska Press Association v. Stuart, 427 U.S. 539, 613 (Brennan, J., concurring).

[145] 216 Va. 800, 805-06, 224 S.E.2d 132, 137 (1976). *See also Fitzgerald,* 691 F.2d 666 (4th Cir. 1982).

[146] 216 Va. at 805-06, 224 S.E.2d at 137.

[147] *Gazette (Fleming),* 229 Va. at 50, 325 S.E.2d at 746.

to eliminate him as a voice of opposition.[148]   This, the court held, was evidence of actual malice.

Virginia courts, it seems, are taking a dim view of inaccuracies published about persons who assume the role of innocent victims. The three negligence cases in the *Gazette* opinion and the *Richmond Newspapers* case demonstrate that the Virginia Supreme Court has a low threshold when determining the existence of fault. While appearing to rely on the "reasonable journalist" definition of negligence, the court seems to be applying a much stricter test. The action by the reporter in *Richmond Newspapers,* in particular, was reasonable.

The court, on the other hand, seems to be applying the actual malice standard with the rigor that the U.S. Supreme Court requires.   Evidence of thorough research before publishing is insulating the media from liability.

THE LIBEL DEFENDANT

A defendant can win a libel action in a number of ways. The defendant, by making a variety of arguments, can attempt to have a case dismissed by the judge before the trial begins. This is called seeking a summary judgment. Arguments for summary judgment can also be made at the completion of the plaintiff's case. At that point, the defendant can argue that the plaintiff has not satisfied all elements of the burden of proof and, therefore, the case should be dismissed. This argument would come after the defendant's attorney has cross-examined the plaintiff's witnesses in an attempt to demonstrate weaknesses in the evidence presented by the plaintiff.

---

[148] 229 Va. at 15, 325 S.E.2d at 725.

A defendant is not required to produce evidence, but if efforts to dismiss a case are unsuccessful, the defendant will almost always do so. That evidence can either attack elements in the plaintiff's case or can advance a defense for the publication. Virginia law provides for three complete defenses for libel: expiration of the statute of limitations, qualified privilege and opinion. The opinion defense can be sub-divided into the publication of pure opinion and the privilege of fair comment and criticism.

Truth is probably a complete defense as well. Since a libel plaintiff must prove the defamatory material is false, if a defendant can introduce evidence that the published material is true, the defendant will win. The Virginia Supreme Court, however, has said that, since the plaintiff must prove falsity, "truth no longer is an affirmative defense to be established by the defendant."[149] But a defendant who wants to advance a defense of truth would almost surely be allowed to do so, particularly since federal courts in Virginia have continued to hold that truth is a complete defense within the commonwealth.[150]

In addition, the developing defenses of good reporting and neutral reporting can protect journalists from some libel verdicts.

Statute of Limitations

When it applies, the statute of limitations defense stops a libel action before the trial begins. Virginia, like most states, only allows recent disputes to be adjudicated. Statutes of limitations provide specific deadlines in which legal actions can be filed.

---

[149] *Id.*

[150] *See* cases cited at *infra* note 198.

The statute of limitations for libel in Virginia is one year, so no libel action can be brought based on a publication that is more than a year old.[151] The clock begins running on a libel action when the publication is generally available to the public, rather than from the copyright date or the date that may appear on the publication.[152]

In addition, the Fourth U.S. Circuit Court of Appeals has held that the single-publication rule applies in Virginia.[153] In essence, the rule prohibits a libel plaintiff from maintaining more than one libel action against the same defendant based on one publication. In the absence of such a rule, a plaintiff could sue the defendant for libel in every circuit in Virginia where the defamatory material was circulated.

Qualified Privilege

The privilege to make certain communications has a long and honorable history in the commonwealth. Early in the Twentieth Century, the Virginia Supreme Court recognized that citizens had a privilege – or right – to comment on matters of public concern, that these commentators should be informed about such matters, and that the conduct of public officers or candidates for public office is a matter of public concern.[154]

Through the years, then, there developed two type of privilege: absolute and qualified.

Absolutely privileged communications are those made in the course of conducting government business. The Virginia Supreme Court has held that it attaches to three classes of

---

[151] Va. Code sec. 8.01-247.1 (1950).

[152] Morrisey v. William Morrow & Co., Inc., 739 F.2d 962, 967-68 (4th Cir. 1984).

[153] *Id.* at 967-68.

[154] *James,* 163 Va. at 877-78, 178 S.E. at 19-20.

communication: (1) proceedings of legislative bodies, (2) judicial proceedings and (3) communications by military and naval officers.[155] As will be demonstrated, it's clear that other types of public proceedings are also privileged. An absolute privilege means that no lawsuits can arise from statements made as part of the official proceedings. A member of the Virginia General Assembly, for example, can say anything from the chamber floor without fear of a defamation action. And a member of a city council or board of supervisors cannot be sued for libel based on comments made during an official meeting. In addition, documents that arise from these official settings are privileged.

Qualified privilege grew out of a recognition that speech on certain matters needed to be protected. Originally, in addition to protection for governmental proceedings, the law also protected "anything said or written by a master in giving the character of a servant who has been in employment."[156] Privilege, then, was specifically designed to attach to communications between persons who owed some duty to each other.

Early in the Twentieth Century, however, the commonwealth recognized that the discussion of public events is important to society. Indeed, there was a duty of sorts between public officials and citizens and between citizens and other citizens related to the conduct of the public's business, justifying the extension of the qualified privilege to reports and discussion of public events. A qualified privilege means that persons reporting on or discussing the events that occur in absolutely privileged forums are protected from libel suits if certain qualifications are met. Those qualifications are that the

---

[155] *Storey,* 202 Va. at 590, 118 S.E.2d at 669.

[156] Penick v. Ratcliffe, 149 Va. 618, 632-34, 140 S.E. 664, 669 (1927), *quoting* Williams Printing Company v. Saunders, 112 Va. 156, 73 S.E. 472.

report must be accurate, it must be fair and it must be made without ill will or spite, that is, without common law malice.

An important corollary to the qualified privilege rule is that, in addition to official proceedings, it attaches to reports taken from public records. The privilege attaches even if the record is in error and, therefore, a report based on the record is in error. Truth or falsity, therefore, is not at issue in such cases. The question is "whether or not the news article was published in good faith and was a substantially correct report of the record. . . ."[157] If the news account is not an accurate representation of what is in the official record, however, the journalist may be held accountable.[158]

Qualified privilege has been held to attach to various reports from sources that were not governmental. For example:

- Statements by a college public information officer to a newspaper reporter about a controversy on campus were conceded by attorneys in the case to be privileged.[159]
- A press release by a plaintiff in a lawsuit stating that the suit had been filed and accurately summarizing the allegations in the suit was held to be privileged.[160]
- A motorist's complaint to a police chief about the conduct of a police officer was held to be privileged.[161]
- Because the law recognizes that privilege attaches to communications between parties who have common interests, communications between employers and

---

[157] *Penick,* 149 Va. at 632, 140 S.E. at 669.

[158] Times-Dispatch Publishing Co., Inc. v. Zoll, 148 Va. 850, 857-59, 139 S.E. 505, 507 (1927).

[159] Sanders v. Harris (Times-World Corporation), 213 Va. 369, 372, 192 S.E.2d 754, 757 (1972).

[160] Bull v. Logetronics, Inc., 323 F. Supp. 115, 135 (E.D. Va. 1971).

[161] Smalls v. Wright, 241 Va. 52, 399 S.E.2d 805 (1991).

employees and among employees in the same company have been held to be privileged.[162]

The qualified privilege defense can be defeated on a showing that the published report was inaccurate, unfair or was made with ill will or spite. Specifically, it may be defeated upon a showing of actual malice, use of intemperate or disproportionate language, deliberate over-exposure of the charges or over-publicity, or gross indifference.[163] It may not be defeated upon a showing of negligence.[164] The official record need not be quoted verbatim, and some minor errors will not defeat the privilege, but the report must be "substantially correct."[165] In addition, if a journalist draws inferences from the report and those inferences are incorrect, the privilege will not stand.[166] Finally, privilege does not extend to official reports of acts by foreign governments.[167]

One additional privilege exists for broadcasters in Virginia. A state law provides that a broadcaster cannot be held responsible for defamatory statements made over the air by someone who does not work for the station. The privilege can be defeated if a plaintiff can show that the broadcaster failed to exercise due care to prevent the broadcast of the defamation. The same statute provides that a broadcaster cannot be held

---

[162] *See, e.g.,* Kroger Company v. Young, 210 Va. 564, 567-68, 172 S.E.2d 720, 722-23 (1970); *Montgomery Ward,* 165 Va. at 378, 182 S.E. at 269-70.

[163] *Great Coastal,* 230 Va. at 153-54, 334 S.E.2d at 853; Southwestern Tidewater Opportunity Project, Inc. v. Bade, 246 Va. 273, 435 S.E.2d 131 (1993).

[164] *Gazette,* 299 Va. at 18, 325 S.E.2d at 727. *See also* Rushford v. The New Yorker Magazine, 846 F.2d 249, 254-55 (4th Cir. 1988).

[165] Alexandria Gazette Corp. v. West, 198 Va. 159, 159, 93 S.E.2d 274, 279 (1956). *See also Rushford,* 846 F.2d at 254-55.

[166] *Times-Dispatch Publishing,* 148 Va. at 858-59, 139 S.E. at 507-08.

[167] Lee v. The Dong-A-Ilbo, 849 F.2d 876, 877-80 (4th Cir. 1988).

liable for defamatory statements made by or on behalf of any candidate for public office under any circumstances.[168]

Opinion

Statements of opinion are protected in one of two ways in Virginia. First, if a statement is considered pure opinion – that is, it cannot be proved to be true or false – it is not considered defamatory and, therefore, is not actionable. Second, if reasonable people can disagree on the truth or falsity of a statement and if the statement is based on facts that are provably true or false, the statement is considered fair comment or criticism and is protected when certain qualifications are met.

Pure Opinion. Virginia protects pure opinion as a category of speech even though the U.S. Supreme Court has ruled that such protection is not necessary under the First Amendment. In *Milkovich v. Lorain Journal*[169] the Court held that statements of opinion are not part of a special category of speech that is automatically protected. However, the Court also noted that a statement cannot be defamatory unless it can be proved to be false.[170] Under *Milkovich,* therefore, statements of opinion are implicitly protected, since they cannot be proved to be false.

The *Milkovich* ruling requires an additional step in libel actions involving opinion. Virginia has circumvented that extra step. In 1985, the Virginia Supreme Court ruled that "pure expressions of opinion, not amounting to 'fighting words' cannot form the basis of an action for defamation."[171] The ruling was based on the First Amendment to the U.S.

---

[168] Va. Code sec. 8.01-49 (1950).

[169] 497 U.S. 1 (1990).

[170] *Id.* at 19-20.

[171] Chaves v. Johnson, 230 Va. 112, 119, 335 S.E.2d 97, 101-02 (1985).

Constitution and on Article 1, sec. 12 of Virginia's Constitution.[172] These two provisions, the court held, "protect the right of the people to teach, preach, write, or speak any such opinion, however ill-founded, without inhibition by actions for libel and slander." Then, quoting from Thomas Jefferson's first inaugural address in 1801, the Virginia court noted that "'error of opinion may be tolerated where reason is left free to combat it.'"[173]

Courts have generally provided protection for opinion on the basis of three distinct rationales: (1) an idea that cannot be false cannot be true and, in a libel action, the constitutional defense of truth would be lost; (2) an opinion carries less authority than a fact and is less likely to threaten the interests and values safeguarded by libel law; and (3) most forms of speech have an affirmative constitutional value, and a rule that chills the expression of opinion is unacceptable.[174]

In addition, implicit in the rulings on opinion is the rationale that, since an opinion cannot be proved to be true or false, it can carry no defamatory meaning – only statements of fact are defamatory; what one believes is not.

The Virginia Supreme Court, for example, has held that to call someone inexperienced is a statement of opinion and, therefore, does not impute unfitness. Noted the court: Many physicians, it is to be hoped, cure their first patients." The court also noted that the characterization, like all statements of opinion, is relative: "A corporal might seem inexperienced to a sergeant, but not to a private. The relative nature of such opinions is obvious to anyone who hears them."[175] The same is

---

[172] Article 1, sec 12 of the Virginia Constitution is quoted at *supra* Chapter 1, note 19.

[173] *Chaves,* 230 Va. at 119, 335 S.E.2d at 102.

[174] Potomac Valve & Fitting, Inc. v. Crawford Fitting Co., 829 F.2d 1280, 1285-86 (4th Cir. 1988).

[175] *Chaves,* 230 Va. at 119, 335 S.E.2d at 101.

true, the court held, with a charge that a person or agency charges excessive fees for its services.[176]

Other statements of opinion, Virginia courts have held, are:

- that a person is discourteous;[177]
- that a charitable organization does not spend a reasonable percent of its total income on program services;[178]
- the statement, "personally I wouldn't trust him as far as I can throw him;"[179]
- the characterization on a radio program that a named person was "the ugliest man in Danville;"[180]
- characterizing the operator of a program to distribute gift packs to service personnel as a "veteran charity entrepreneur" who charged "hefty" markups for the gift packs;[181]
- a criticism that a contractor would not finish a road on time because of the contractor's past performance;[182]
- a statement that there was a problem with an auto dealership's sales manager who either did not know about a credit fraud problem or did nothing about the problem.[183]

On the other hand, the Virginia Supreme Court determined that, while statements about sexual harassment might be statements of opinion, a statement that a person

---

[176] *Id.*

[177] *Auvil,* 10 Media L. Rep. (BNA) at 2303.

[178] *National Foundation for Cancer Research,* 705 F.2d at 100-01.

[179] Lapkoff v. Wilks, 696 F.2d 78, 82 (4th Cir. 1992).

[180] Motsinger v. Kelly, 11 Media L. Rep. (BNA) 2459, 2460 (Circuit Court, City of Danville, August 12, 1985).

[181] *Chapin,* 993F.2d at 1093-94.

[182] *James,* 163 Va. at 884, 178 S.E. at 22.

[183] *Lapkoff,* 969 F.2d at 82-83.

received negative performance evaluations because of the person's responses to so-called sexual harassment was a statement of fact,[184] as was calling a person who crossed a picket line a traitor.[185]

In libel actions, the responsibility is upon the court, rather than a jury, to determine whether a statement is one of fact or opinion.[186]

Fair Comment & Criticism. Fair comment and criticism is a qualified privilege that protects commentary based on statements of fact. In 1935, the Virginia Supreme Court explained the rationale behind the privilege:

> The privilege or right of a citizen to comment on matters of public concern is based upon a sound public policy, i.e., the public should be informed of the character, qualifications, actions, and conduct of public officers and candidates for public offices, and other matters of public nature. . . . The comment or criticism in such cases may reflect upon the plaintiff in his public actions or conduct; indeed, he would not complain unless they tended in some degree to defame or ridicule him. Sound public policy requires that immunity should be granted to newspapers and other citizens in the discussion of public affairs and where the comment or stricture is based upon established facts, an action does not lie unless there is proof of. . . malice, or the language used

---

[184] Williams v. Garraghty, 249 Va. 224, 233, 455 S.E.2d 209, 215 (1995).

[185] Old Dominion Branch 496 v. Austin, 213 Va. 377, 384, 192 S.E.2d 737, 742 (1972), *rev'd* 418 U.S. 264 (1974). *See* discussion accompanying *infra* notes 190-92.

[186] *Chaves,* 230 Va. at 119, 335 S.E.2d at 102.

so exceeds reasonable limits that malice may be inferred therefrom.[187]

For the defense to succeed in Virginia, therefore, the comment (1) must be on matters of public concern, (2) must be based upon statements of fact that are accurately stated, and (3) must be made without common law malice, that is, without ill will, hatred or spite. Courts in many jurisdictions also require that the comment expressed be the genuine opinion of the publisher of the comment. That is, the comment or criticism must be the expression of the publisher's opinion, it cannot be a news account relating the opinion of another. While this element has not been explicitly adopted in Virginia, it appears to be implicit the court's rulings.

Fair comment and criticism is often easier to define than to apply. In one Virginia case, for example, a court held that criticism of a fund-raising agency for not spending enough of its income on program services was a statement of opinion and protected.[188] To report that a bank was near insolvency, however, was a statement of fact rather than opinion, even though the statement was an interpretation based upon an analysis of the bank's holdings.[189]

One of the most famous disagreements over whether a statement was opinion or fact grew out of a Virginia case that was ultimately settled by the U.S. Supreme Court. The case began during a labor dispute. A non-union post office employee complained about being identified in a union newsletter as a "scab."[190] When he asked for a definition of the

---

[187] *James,* 163 Va. at 878, 178 S.E. at 20.

[188] *National Foundation for Cancer Research,* 705 F.2d at 100.

[189] *Blue Ridge Bank,* 866 F.2d at 865.

[190] *Old Dominion Branch,* 213 Va. at 378-79, 192 S.E.2d 738-39.

word "scab," the newsletter published the following, which is often attributed to Jack London:

> After God had finished the rattlesnake, the toad, and the vampire, He had some awful substance left with which he made a scab.
>
> A scab is a two-legged animal with a corkscrew soul, a water brain, a combination backbone of jelly and glue. Where others have hearts, he carries a tumor of rotten principles.
>
> When a scab comes down the street, men turn their backs and Angels weep in Heaven, and the Devil shuts the gates of hell to keep him out.
>
> No man (or woman) has a right to scab so long as there is a pool of water to drown his carcass in, or a rope long enough to hang his body with. Judas was a gentleman compared with a scab. For betraying his Master, he had character enough to hang himself. A scab has not.
>
> Essau sold his birthright for a mess of pottage. Judas sold his Savior for thirty pieces of silver. Benedict Arnold sold his country for a promise of a commission in the British Army. The scab sells his birthright, country, his wife, his children and his fellowmen for an unfulfilled promise from his employer.
>
> Essau was a traitor to himself; Judas was a traitor to God; Benedict Arnold was a traitor to his country, a SCAB is a traitor to his god, his country, his family and his class.[191]

---

[191] 213 Va. at 379, 192 S.E.2d at 739.

The Virginia Supreme Court ruled that identifying persons who crossed picket lines as traitors of such low character and rotten principles that they should be despised by their fellow workers was not a statement of opinion and, therefore, was not protected by the First Amendment.[192]

The U.S. Supreme Court, however, reversed the ruling, holding that the piece consisted of "rhetorical hyperbole" and was "a lusty and imaginative expression of contempt felt by union members towards those who refuse to join."[193] No one, the Court noted, would reasonably believe that there was a charge of the criminal offense of treason.[194]

Truth

Truth has long been recognized as a complete defense for defamation.[195]

In 1986, however, the U.S. Supreme Court made explicit what had been implicit in libel law since its landmark ruling in *New York Times Co. v. Sullivan.* In *Times,* of course, the Court ruled that actual malice was defined as "knowledge of falsity," the implication being that there must be falsity before there can be "knowledge" of the falsity. In *Philadelphia Newspapers v. Hepps,* the Court stated explicitly that falsity must be proved by the plaintiff in libel actions when the subject of the allegedly defamatory material relates to matters of public concern.[196]

The ruling, and the implicit collateral holding that the negligence of false statements must also be proved, prompted

---

[192] 213 Va. at 384, 192 S.E.2d at 742.

[193] Letter Carriers v. Austin, 418 U.S. 264, 286 (1974). The name of the case changed when it was decided by the U.S. Supreme Court.

[194] *Id.* at 285.

[195] *See, e.g., Chaffin,* 84 Va. at 113, 1 S.E. at 807.

[196] 475 U.S. 767 (1986).

the Virginia Supreme Court, as indicated previously, to hold that truth is no longer a defense. Since the plaintiff is required to prove falsity in order to establish the negligence of such falsity, the state supreme court reasoned, "truth is no longer an affirmative defense to be established by the defendant."[197]

The ruling is probably more semantic than precedential, however. It is inconceivable that a defendant in a libel action would not be allowed to defend on the ground that the defamatory statement is true. In addition, even in the face of the state supreme court's ruling, the federal appellate courts in Virginia have continued to hold to the tenet that truth is a complete defense in libel actions.[198]

When truth has been pleaded in libel actions, the court has held that slight inaccuracies will not cause the defense to fail. So long as the defamatory charge is true in substance, the defense will stand.[199]

Good Reporting, Neutral Reporting

A couple of developing defenses should be mentioned before discussion of the defendant's case is closed. The defenses of good reporting and fair report have not been explicitly applied in Virginia, but have been implied in a number of court cases.

Good Reporting. The defense grows out of the Supreme Court's pronouncement that no libel plaintiff may

---

[197] *Gazette,* 229 Va. at 15, 325 S.E.2d at 725.

[198] *See, e.g.,* Chapin v. Greve, 787 F. Supp. at 563; *McBride,* 871 F. Supp. at 891-92; Bills v. Sunshine Wireless Co., 824 F. Supp. 60, 64 (E.D. Va. 1993); Seabolt v. Westmoreland Coal Co., 703 F. Supp. 1235, 1242 (W.D. Va. 1989), *aff'd* 989 F.2d 144 (4th Cir. 1990), *cert. denied* 498 U.S. 848 (1990).

[199] *Saleeby,* 197 Va. at 763, 91 S.E.2d at 407.

prevail without showing some degree of fault[200] and a Virginia statute providing that a showing of proper investigation, reliability of sources and absence of negligence would mitigate damages.[201] The defense is based on the presumption that if there is no showing of negligence, there can be no showing of fault of any kind, and the defendant will prevail. Since negligence is the minimum degree of fault, no greater degree of fault can exist if the minimum degree does not exist.

To demonstrate an absence of negligence, a news organization must demonstrate that it properly investigated the defamatory allegations before publishing. This means contacting all relevant persons involved in the controversy, particularly the subject of the defamation, using documents when possible, quoting accurately and clearly following the guidelines of responsible reporting.[202] Basically it means providing a good faith effort to be accurate and fair.

Neutral Reporting. The defense provides protection for a news organization reporting on the government. It allows the organization to report, without liability, defamatory statements that do not originate in privileged sources, even if the organization knows the statements are false, if those statements are based on government actions or reports.[203] Generally, any statements relating to matters affecting public welfare or public interest might fall into the fair report privilege.[204] Indeed, some jurisdictions have applied the fair

---

[200] *Gertz,* 418 U.S. at 347-48.

[201] Va. Code sec. 8-01-48 (1950).

[202] *See, e.g.,* HOPKINS, *Negligence, supra* note 118, at 18-20.

[203] *Reuber,* 925 F.2d at 712.

[204] 925 F.2d at 713.

report privilege to any statements made by well-known persons or organizations not part of the government.[205]

The Fourth U.S. Circuit Court of Appeals, which has jurisdiction over Virginia, has accepted the fair report privilege as a defense, but did so in a Maryland case. The privilege has not been applied in a Virginia case, but the Fourth Circuit case might prompt the state court to consider the privilege for the state.

Mitigating Damages

Virginia law provides that a defendant may mitigate damages by offering an apology to the plaintiff[206] or by producing evidence showing that the news story was responsibly investigated, written and published.[207] The viability of this last statute under modern libel law is in question, however. Since the U.S. Supreme Court has required all libel plaintiffs to prove some degree of fault in order to win their cases, a showing that there is no negligence will usually be sufficient for a libel defendant to win. Negligence is based directly on how a story was investigated, written and published, and since a showing that there is no negligence is sufficient for a defendant to win, the statute may have little meaning today.

---

[205] Edwards v. National Audubon Society, Inc., 556 F.2d 113 (2d Cir. 1977), *cert. denied sub nom.* Edwards v. New York Times Co., 434 U.S. 1002 (1977). *See also Reuber,* 925 F.2d at 712-13.

[206] Va. Code sec. 8.01-46 (1950).

[207] Va. Code sec. 8.01-48 (1950).

Chapter 5

PRIVATE PEOPLE, PRIVATE PLACES AND PEACE OF MIND

Invasion of privacy is a relatively recent but an emotion-charged area of the law. The publication of some secret tidbit or a camera probing into private places can bring the most vociferous denunciations of the media. Few publications raise the ire of the public more than a photograph of a grieving mother or a story about events from a person's private life.

Partly because of the high emotions associated with the conflict between a person's private life and newsgathering, a body of law has developed in the United States to protect the privacy rights of individuals. That body of law was first explored in detail by William Prosser in 1965 as part of the American Law Institute's *Restatement of the Law* series.[1] In the *Restatement (Second) of Torts,* Prosser identified four types of

---

[1] Invasion of privacy traces its heritage to 1890 when Samuel Warren and Louis Brandeis published "The Right of Privacy" in the *Harvard Law Review.* Prosser, however, was first to systematically examine the law of invasion of privacy and delineate the four separate invasion of privacy torts. See RESTATEMENT (SECOND) OF TORTS, sec. 652A, comment a (1977). The RESTATEMENT is now in its second edition.

invasion of privacy: appropriation, intrusion, publication of private information and false light invasion of privacy.[2]

Since then, a number of states have sifted out some of these torts. North Carolina and Ohio, for example, do not allow lawsuits to be brought under the tort of false light invasion of privacy.[3] Virginia has gone even further: The commonwealth recognizes only appropriation, and only twice have appellate courts in Virginia resolved appropriation cases.[4]

This does not mean that Virginia lawmakers have no regard for the privacy and peace of mind of individuals, however. Indeed, vestiges of intrusion, false light and publication of private information appear in a variety of forms in Virginia law. The commonwealth has also made ample effort to protect the privacy or peace of mind of its citizens through statutes prohibiting insulting words, the intentional infliction of emotional distress, trespassing and the like. In addition, in 1976 the Virginia General Assembly passed the Privacy Protection Act, which doesn't protect privacy, but regulates the way information about individuals is collected, manipulated and disseminated. The act focuses on data collection agencies rather than the dissemination of information by the individuals or the media. It gives individuals the right of access to information collected about them.[5] Indeed, in 2001 the General

---

[2] RESTATEMENT (SECOND) OF TORTS, sec. 652A (1977). Hereinafter cited as RESTATEMENT.

[3] *See* Renwick v. News and Observer Publishing Co., 310 N.C. 312, 312 S.E.2d 405 (1981), and Rinehart v. Toledo Blade Co., 21 Ohio App. 3d 274, 487 N.E.2d 920 (1985).

[4] *See* Falwell v. Penthouse International, Ltd., 521 F. Supp. 1204 (W.D. Va. 1981) and Town & Country Properties, Inc. v. Riggins, 249 Va. 387, 457 S.E.2d 356 (1995). The two appropriation cases are discussed at *infra* notes 12-13 and 16-18.

[5] *See* Va. Code secs. 2.1-377 - 2.1-386 (1950).

Assembly changed the name of the act to the Government Data Collection and Dissemination Practices Act.[6]

Many of these statutes are not typically regarded as "invasion of privacy" statutes, but since their design is to protect the privacy, dignity or peace of mind of individuals, they will be addressed in this chapter, along with a passel of related issues.

APPROPRIATION

Appropriation is the use of a person's name, image or likeness for commercial gain without permission.[7] In Virginia an appropriation suit may be brought by:

> any person whose name, portrait, or picture is used without having first obtained the written consent of such person, or if dead, of the surviving consort and if none, of the next of kin, or if a minor, the written consent of his or her parent or guardian, for advertising purposes or for the purposes of trade.[8]

The statute allows a suit to be brought up until twenty years after the death of the person whose name or image is used.

The Virginia Supreme Court has construed the state's appropriation statute as granting a property right to individuals.[9]

---

[6] Va. Legis. 844 (2001).

[7] RESTATEMENT, sec. 652C.

[8] Va. Code sec. 8.01-40 (1950).

[9] Lavery v. Automation Management Consultants, Inc., 234 Va. 145, 360 S.E.2d 336 (1987).

That is, according to the court a person's name, likeness or image is tantamount to a piece of property, and only the individual can benefit from the use of that property. Therefore, an action for appropriation "is an action for invasion of. . . 'property' rights and not one for 'injury to the person.'"[10]

Appropriation most often applies to advertising, where images of the beautiful or well-known are used to sell products. One had best have the permission of Michael Jordan before putting his photograph on a box of Wheaties or in an advertisement for Nike basketball shoes, for example.

Appropriation can also apply to free-lance photographers and writers, however, who make their livings selling information or images. Virtually any time a free-lance photographer sells a photo to a newspaper or magazine, for example, the photographer has used the likeness of a person for commercial gain and, often, without permission.

So why are these photographers not liable for appropriation?

They aren't sued because courts generally recognize newsworthiness as a sufficient defense for appropriation. But newsworthiness is not always easy to prove.

A free-lance photographer covering a major football game at Virginia Tech, for example, would probably not be guilty of appropriation for selling to *Sports Illustrated* a photo he took of Michael Vick who happened to be in the stands watching the game. There is little likelihood an appropriation suit would stand even if the magazine ran the photo on its cover. Both the game and Vick's appearance at the game are newsworthy. A person not as well-known as Vick, however, might not be newsworthy and, under some circumstances, might

---

[10] 234 Va. at 154, 360 S.E.2d at 341-42.

be the subject of a successful appropriation suit.[11] In addition, if the photograph of Vick appeared on the cover of a program for a subsequent Virginia Tech football game, and if Vick had not given his permission for the use, both the photographer and the university might be guilty of appropriation.

The primary difference between the two cases is that *Sports Illustrated* is in the business of disseminating information and ideas, an activity protected by the First Amendment. The primary reason the university would sell programs, on the other hand, is to make money, not to disseminate information.

Appropriation	
Tort: Use of a person's name, image or likeness, without permission, for commercial gain.	*Remedy in Virginia:* Appropriation Statute

The importance of this distinction was demonstrated in a 1981 case in the U.S. District Court for the Western District of Virginia. Evangelist Jerry Falwell attempted to halt distribution of the March 1981 issue of *Penthouse* magazine because it contained an interview he had given two free-lance journalists. When his attempt failed, he brought suit against *Penthouse* claiming a variety of wrongs, including false light invasion of privacy and appropriation.

---

[11] There are no Virginia cases on this point, *but see* Arrington v. New York Times Co., 55 N.Y.2d 433, 449 N.Y.S.2d 941 (1982), *cert. denied* 459 U.S. 1146 (1983).

A federal court dismissed the false light claim, noting that the cause of action does not exist under Virginia law.[12] The court recognized that the interview was published in *Penthouse* for the purpose of commercial gain, but noted that "everything that appears in a magazine is placed with the intention of increasing sales." To construe the appropriation rule so broadly that it would cover such a case, the court held, would conflict with "important constitutional freedoms, which guarantee the uninhibited dissemination of ideas."[13]

A Richmond judge, however, interpreted the statute just that broadly in March 1998 when he ruled that an appropriation suit based on a novel could go to trial. The parents of two people killed at an Interstate 64 rest stop in September 1989 sued Patricia Cornwell for invasion of privacy, claiming that details in Cornwell's 1992 novel *All That Remains* were based, in part, on autopsies conducted on the bodies of their children. Recognizing that Virginia only allows an invasion of privacy suit when the likeness of a person is used without permission for advertising or trade purposes, Judge Melvin R. Hughes Jr. ruled that the parents could attempt to prove to a jury that the descriptions in the novel were for advertising or trade purposes.[14] Nine months later, however, Judge Hughes dismissed the privacy claim, ruling that the events in the novel differed from the details of the actual killings and that Cornwell's characters are fictitious.[15]

A real estate firm also claimed to use the name of a celebrity for information rather than advertising purposes, but the Virginia Supreme Court did not buy the claim. In 1991,

---

[12] *Falwell*, 521 F. Supp. at 1206.

[13] *Id.* at 1210. *See also* Falwell v. Flynt, 797 F.2d 1270, 1278 (4th Cir. 1986), *rev'd on other grounds*, 485 U.S. 46 (1988).

[14] Alan Cooper, *Invasion of Privacy Lawsuit Against Cornwell to Proceed*, RICHMOND TIMES-DISPATCH, March 2, 1998, B1.

[15] *Metro In Brief*, WASHINGTON POST, December 16, 1998, B3.

Hall of Fame football player John Riggins was divorced from Mary Lou Riggins. Later that year Mrs. Riggins, a real estate broker, placed on the market the house she had acquired as part of the divorce settlement, and made the sale known with a flyer that advertised the house as being Riggins' former home. The house was in Northern Virginia where Riggins, a former member of the Washington Redskins football team, was well known. Riggins, who received fees for personal appearances and for lending his name to advertising ventures, sued for appropriation and won more than $53,000 in damages.[16]

The real estate company argued that it should not be required to pay damages for the disclosure of truthful, public information. The identity of Riggins' ownership of the property "is an immutable characteristic" of the property, the company argued, and the information was freely available to the public from Fairfax County land records.[17]

The state supreme court disagreed. The flyer was clearly advertising material, the court held, and Riggins' name was used to enhance the probability of ultimate sale of the property. Therefore, the court concluded that the name was used for advertising purposes, as specifically forbidden by state law.[18]

Appropriation, therefore, is not purely an invasion of privacy tort, though it is recognized as such in most states. Regardless of legal distinctions, however, appropriation may be used in Virginia to protect the image or likeness of a person from unauthorized use.

---

[16] Town & Country Properties, Inc. v. Riggins, 249 Va. 387, 391-93, 457 S.E.2d 356, 358-60 (1995).

[17] 249 Va. at 393-94, 457 S.E.2d at 361-62.

[18] 249 Va. at 395, 457 S.E.2d at 362-63.

INTRUSION

Intrusion occurs when a place where a person has a reasonable expectation of privacy is physically invaded. The tort has nothing to do with publication; the invasion occurs because of electronic eavesdropping, the use of high-powered photographic lenses to snoop into a person's back yard, peeping through a bedroom window or similar activities.

Virginia does not recognize intrusion as an invasion of privacy tort in either statutory or common law, but that doesn't mean Virginia law allows journalists – or anyone else – free access to homes, businesses and other places individuals could ordinarily expect privacy. A bundle of Virginia statutes protect privacy in such places. Indeed, Virginia legislators have expressed their attitude toward the significance of the privacy of the home:

> It is hereby declared that the protection and preservation of the home is the keystone of democratic government; that the public health and welfare and the good order of the community require that members of the community enjoy in their homes a feeling of well-being, tranquility, and privacy, and when absent from their homes carry with them the sense of security inherent in the assurance that they may return to the enjoyment of their homes.[19]

That declaration accompanies a state law that prohibits the picketing of any residence or home "in a manner which disrupts or threatens to disrupt any individual's right to tranquility in his home."[20] The law is not necessarily designed to protect a person from physical intrusion, but is certainly aimed at protecting peace of mind. Another law with a similar design prohibits the use of pre-recorded telephone sales calls

---

[19] Va. Code sec. 18.2-418 (1950).
[20] Va. Code sec. 18.2-419 (1950).

that do not disconnect when the person called hangs up the phone.[21]

And a law that cuts across both intents – peace of mind and protection from intrusion – might be Virginia's prohibition against the burning of a cross on private property, if the burning is done with an intent to intimidate any person.[22]

Intrusion	
Tort: The physical invasion of a place where a person has a reasonable expectation of privacy.	*Remedy in Virginia:* Prohibition Against Picketing Residences "Peeping Tom" Statute Trespassing Statutes

At least two other statutes also protect individual privacy in a manner related to intrusion. What is often called a "peeping Tom" statute prohibits any person from going onto private property for the purpose of secretly looking into a dwelling. The law applies to both permanent structures – like houses and apartment complexes – and temporary structures – like tents or motor homes.[23] A second statute prohibits the photographing or filming, without permission, of any person who is partially clothed or nude and who is in a place where the person "would have a reasonable expectation of privacy."[24]

---

[21] Va. Code sec. 18.2-425.1 (1950).

[22] Va. Code sec. 18.2-423 (1950). In June 2001, when this book was going to press, the cross-burning statute was being challenged in the Virginia Supreme Court. *See* discussion of Black v. Commonwealth in Chapter 3.

[23] Va. Code sec. 18.2-130 (1950).

[24] Va. Code sec. 18.2-386.1 (1950).

Trespassing laws are among the most common methods of protecting an individual's right to the private enjoyment of home or business. Virginia trespassing laws prohibit a person from going onto or remaining on private property after having been forbidden to do so.[25] The order may be oral or in writing. Therefore, a person is guilty of a misdemeanor when the person goes onto property that has a sign posted warning people to stay away.

If no sign is visible, a person can presume that permission to enter property has been given and may go upon that property. The person must leave when ordered to do so by the owner or custodian of the property, however. In addition, the Virginia Supreme Court has ruled that trespassing statutes apply to public as well as private property.[26] Specific statutes also make it a crime to enter a school, church or cemetery without permission.[27]

How do the trespassing statutes apply to journalists and photographers?

Trespassing statutes protect the privacy of individuals only from the actual presence of others. That is, the law prohibits individuals from going places where they are not wanted, when those places are under the legal control of others. The law does not protect the privacy of individuals if their activity may be witnessed from public property.

Therefore, a person is allowed to stand on a public sidewalk and witness any activity occurring on private property. The witness may write about what is seen or heard and, indeed, may photograph anything visible. But, while no Virginia cases speak to the point, the witness is likely to encounter legal

---

[25] Va. Code sec. 18.2-119 (1950).

[26] Johnson et al. v. Commonwealth, 212 Va. 579, 186 S.E.2d 53 (1972), *cert. denied,* 407 U.S. 295 (1972). The case involved a group of students convicted of trespassing after demonstrating at Madison College.

[27] Va. Code secs. 18.2-125 , 18.2-128 and 18.2-129 (1950).

problems by using special photographic or sound equipment to record activity on private property that could not be seen or heard from public property. Wire tapping or electronic eavesdropping, of course, are prohibited by both state and federal statutes. The Virginia wire tapping law allows the tape recording of telephone conversations if one party to the conversation is aware that it is being recorded.[28]

Newsworthy events often occur on private property – whether that property is the home of an individual or a shopping mall owned by a conglomerate. When those events occur, journalists may presume that they have a license to enter the property. They may also presume they have a right to record what they see and hear. When ordered to leave the property by its owner or custodian, however, again, whether that property is a home or a shopping mall, they are in danger of facing criminal and civil charges if they remain.[29]

The law requires the journalists to leave property when ordered. Nothing in the law, however, prohibits journalists or photographers from recording what they can as they leave. If a law enforcement officer orders a photographer to stop taking pictures, however, certain additional statutes may apply. A variety of Virginia laws require citizens to obey orders of law enforcement officers in their attempts to, among other things, preserve the peace.[30] A photographer could conceivably be

---

[28] Va. Code sec. 19.2-62 (1950).

[29] *See, e.g.,* Hall v. Commonwealth, 188 Va. 72, 49 S.E.2d 369 (1948), in which several Jehovah's Witnesses were arrested for trespassing after being told not to hand out pamphlets at Monroe Terrace Apartments in Richmond. The convictions were upheld.

[30] *See, e.g.,* Va. Code sec. 18.2-463 (1950), which makes it a crime to refuse to help an officer in the execution of his office, and Va. Code sec. 18.2-464 (1950), which makes it a crime to fail to obey an order of a conservator of the peace.

charged under one of these statutes by an officer who argued that the continued activities of the photographer disrupted the peace.

Conversely, two Virginia statutes give journalists a special privilege of access to emergency scenes, even when other citizens must stay away. The statutes allow members of the press to cross police or fire perimeters to cover fires, accidents or other emergency situations.[31] The statutes explicitly prohibit reporters from obstructing police or emergency personnel and implicitly allow the officers to remain in control of the scene, with the power to order members of the press to leave should their presence cause problems.

Ostensibly, these statutes are at odds with trespassing statutes. What happens when an emergency occurs on private property? Virginia law allows reporters to cross police barricades to cover the events, but also allows the owner of the property to order the journalists to leave.

The Virginia Supreme Court has not been required to decide such a case so there is no way of knowing how these competing rights would be balanced. A good rule of thumb for journalists, however, is to obey law enforcement officers and abide by the law.

INTENTIONAL INFLICTION OF EMOTIONAL DISTRESS

Intentional infliction of emotional distress is a relatively recent tort, as it is applied to the media at any rate. It occurs when someone "by extreme and outrageous conduct intentionally or recklessly causes severe emotional distress to another."[32]

---

[31] Va. Code secs. 15.2-1714 and 27-15.1 (1950).
[32] RESTATEMENT, sec. 46.

Intentional infliction, therefore, prompts some of the same reactions – outrage, embarrassment, distress – as some of the torts that fall under the broad umbrella generally assigned to invasion of privacy.

False light invasion of privacy, for example, is the publicizing of false material that, while not defamatory, might embarrass or enrage an individual.[33] A false light suit is not brought to recover for a damaged reputation, therefore, but to recover from the embarrassment or outrage caused by the publication. An intentional infliction suit may be brought for those same reasons.

Similarly, the publication of private information causes distress because material that should be hidden from public view is suddenly given undue publicity.[34] The suit is brought because of the distress caused by the publication of the private material.

False Light Invasion of Privacy	
Tort: The publicizing of false information that may embarrass or enrage a person.	*Remedy in Virginia:* Intentional Infliction of Emotional Distress Insulting Words Statute

Since these torts are not recognized in Virginia, a suit for intentional infliction of emotional distress, depending upon the circumstances, may be substituted, even though intentional infliction is synonymous with neither of them. In addition, the burden of proof for an intentional infliction suit does not match that of any invasion of privacy torts. All four torts require some

---

[33] *Id.* at sec. 652C.
[34] *Id.* at sec. 652D.

degree of outrageousness, however, so substitution is not an unlikely prospect.

In Virginia, a plaintiff in an intentional infliction suit must meet a four-point burden of proof.[35] The plaintiff must prove:

(1) that the conduct on the part of the defendant was intentional or reckless;

(2)   that the conduct offends generally accepted standards of decency or morality;

(3) that the conduct caused emotional distress;

(4) that the emotional distress was severe.

In addition, a plaintiff who is a public figure or a public official must prove that the publication was made with actual malice, that is, with knowledge of falsity or with reckless disregard for the truth.[36]

The *Restatement of Torts* summarizes the intentional infliction test this way:

> Liability has been found only where the conduct has been so outrageous in character, and so extreme in degree, as to go beyond all possible bounds of decency, and to be regarded as atrocious, and utterly intolerable in a civilized community.   Generally, the case is one in which the recitation of the facts to an average member of the community would arouse his resentment against the actor, and lead him to exclaim, "Outrageous!"[37]

In cases involving the media, intentional infliction has been found when a magazine published a sexually explicit classified advertisement giving the name and address of a

---

[35] Womack v. Eldridge, 215 Va. 338, 342, 210 S.E.2d 145, 148 (1974).

[36] Hustler Magazine v. Falwell, 485 U.S. 46, 56 (1988).

[37] RESTATEMENT, sec. 46, comment d.

woman who did not place the ad,[38] when a team physician wrongly reported that a pro football player had a fatal disease,[39] when a photographer obsessively followed Jacqueline Kennedy Onassis and her children,[40] and when a television news team followed paramedics into a private home and filmed unsuccessful efforts to resuscitate a heart-attack victim.[41]

There was no outrageous conduct, however, in the publication of the name and address of the sole witness to an armed robbery and murder,[42] in the publication of names listed in a report on organized crime,[43] in the publication of a story and photographs about children suffocating in a discarded refrigerator,[44] or in the publication of the identity and photograph of an undercover narcotics officer.[45]

Publication of Private Information	
Tort: The publicizing of private information.	*Remedy in Virginia:* None.

---

[38] Vesco v. New Way Enterprises, Ltd., 130 Cal. Rptr. 86, 60 Cal. App. 3d 582 (1976).

[39] Chuy v. Philadelphia Eagles Football Club, 431 F. Supp. 254 (D. Pa. 1977).

[40] Galella v. Onassis, 487 F.2d 986 (2d Cir. 1973).

[41] Miller v. National Broadcasting Co., 232 Cal. Rptr. 668, 187 Cal. App. 3d 1463 (1986).

[42] Hood v. Naeter Brothers Publishing Co., 562 S.W.2d 770 (Mo. App. 1978).

[43] Kilgore v. Younger, 30 Cal. 3d 770, 640 P.2d 793 (1982).

[44] Costlow v. Cusimano, 44 A.D.2d 196, 311 N.Y.S.2d 92 (1970).

[45] Ross v. Burns, 612 F.2d 271 (6th Cir. 1980).

One of the best examples of intentional infliction of emotional distress is *Hustler Magazine v. Falwell*,[46] which was tried in U.S. District Court in Roanoke and eventually made its way to the U.S. Supreme Court.

Hustler published a parody of a Campari Liquor advertisement in which the Rev. Jerry Falwell was portrayed as saying that his first sexual experience was a drunken encounter with his mother in an outhouse. The Campari Liquor campaign involved celebrities describing their first experiences drinking the liquor. Double entendre, however, implied that the celebrities were describing their first sexual encounters.

Larry Flynt, the publisher of *Hustler,* testified at trial that one purpose of the parody was to portray Falwell as a liar, glutton and hypocrite and to assassinate his integrity.[47] Falwell testified that he had never been as angry or as deeply wounded by any publication. He testified that he had never physically attacked anyone, but, when he saw the publication, "I really think that at that moment if Larry Flynt had been nearby I might have physically reacted."[48]

The jury found that the parody was published with an intent to cause severe emotional distress and that it did, indeed, cause such distress.

The U.S. Supreme Court overturned the verdict on other grounds. Though not disturbing the finding that the publication was outrageous or that Falwell had suffered severe emotional distress, the Court held that a public figure must prove actual malice in order to win a suit for intentional infliction of emotional distress.[49] The Court's ruling also indicated that

---

[46] At the circuit court level the case was Falwell v. Flynt, 797 F.2d 1270 (4th Cir. 1986).

[47] *Falwell,* 797 F.2d at 1273.

[48] 797 F.2d at 1276.

[49] *Hustler Magazine,* 485 U.S. at 56. Actual malice, which is defined as knowledge of falsity or reckless disregard for the truth, New York Times

there must be an effort on the part of the plaintiff to pass off as the truth material that is false, and, since the parody could not be reasonably construed as being true, there could be no liability.[50]

INSULTING OR ABUSIVE LANGUAGE

As previously indicated, intentional infliction of emotional distress might be used as a substitute for various invasion of privacy torts, including false light invasion of privacy. Virginia's insulting words and abusive language statutes may be used in the same way.

False light invasion of privacy occurs when false material, which is often insulting, is published about an individual. An insulting words or abusive language suit may be brought when something false and insulting is said *to* a person.

The chapter on libel points out that a suit for insulting words is treated "precisely as an action for slander or libel for words actionable per se, with one exception, namely, no publication is necessary."[51] The state supreme court, however, has also indicated that the insulting words statute continues to provide the means for a cause of action when non-defamatory words "tend to violence and breach of peace," that is, when they are fighting words.[52] Words are actionable, therefore, if they would tend to cause an immediate violent response or a breach

---

Co. v. Sullivan, 376 U.S. 254, 271 (1964), is discussed in detail in Chapter 4.

[50] 485 U.S. at 57.

[51] Carwile v. Richmond Newspapers, 196 Va. 1, 6, 82 S.E.2d 588, 591 (1954).

[52] Allen & Rocks, Inc. v. Dowell, 252 Va. 439, 477 S.E.2d 741 (1996).

of the peace.[53]   It is not necessary for those words to be published or to be defamatory.

Similarly, under Virginia law a person may not use abusive language to another in public. The law provides that a person may not "in the presence or hearing of another, curse or abuse such other person, or use any violent abusive language to such person concerning himself or any of his relations. . . ."[54] The statute has been held to be constitutional by the Virginia Court of Appeals.[55]

---

[53] Va. Code sec. 8.01-45 (1950).

[54] Va. Code sec. 18.2-416 (1950).

[55] Perkins v. Commonwealth, 12 Va. App. 7, 402 S.E.2d 229 (1991).

Chapter 6

ACCESS TO PUBLIC MEETINGS AND OFFICIAL DOCUMENTS

The Virginia General Assembly adopted the state's Freedom of Information Act in 1968 ". . .to ensure the people of this Commonwealth ready access to records in the custody of public officials and free entry to meetings of public bodies wherein the business of the people is being conducted." That's because, legislators wrote, "The affairs of government are not intended to be conducted in an atmosphere of secrecy since at all times the public is to be the beneficiary of any action taken at any level of government."[1]

To help ensure openness, then, the law "to be liberally construed to promote an increased awareness by all persons of governmental activities and afford every opportunity to citizens to witness the operations of government." And any exceptions or exemptions "shall be narrowly construed in order that no thing which should be public may be hidden from any person."[2]

The law, then, requires that citizens be allowed access to records and documents related to the conduct of public business and to meetings of official bodies. The law is not a press law, but a citizen's law, premised on the philosophy that citizens

---

[1] Va. Code sec. 2.1-340.1 (1950).

[2] *Id.*

have a right to know how their business is being conducted. For that reason, there are no prerequisites for access. A citizen has a right to see official records or attend public meetings without tendering reasons.

In addition, since the law is to be liberally construed and exceptions are to be narrowly construed, legal interpretations are to weigh in favor of citizens.

Access is not absolute, however. Some records may be kept from public scrutiny, some business may be conducted behind closed doors, and the act does not apply to some agencies – the Virginia Parole Board, the Virginia State Crime Commission, petit juries, grand juries and, significantly, to informal meetings of members of the Virginia General Assembly.

In addition, lawmakers fiddle with the Freedom of Information Act during almost every session of the general assembly. The last attempt to streamline the act came in 1999, when a number of changes were made. The act remains cumbersome, however, and some of its restrictions board on absurdity. For example, the records portion of the act allows the Department of Game and Inland Fisheries to keep secret the subscription list for its magazine *Virginia Wildlife*. The exemption was added when a constituent complained to her legislator that she didn't want her name disseminated to companies that might use it for solicitations. The legislator was able to get the exemption added to the act.[3]

The Freedom of Information Act, then, is becoming increasingly complex as lawmakers attach provisos, limitations and exceptions. In addition, rulings by the Virginia Supreme Court, which has never indicated genuine concern for the public's right to know, have weakened the act.

---

[3] Del. Jay DeBoer, "Open Government: What Part Do Executive Sessions Play?" a public forum sponsored by the League of Women Voters of Montgomery County, 23 March 1998. See Va. Code sec.2.1-342.01(A)(51).

FREEDOM OF INFORMATION ADVISORY COUNCIL

Clifton A. Woodrum, Chair Virginia House of Delegates	E.M. Miller Jr. Division of Legislative Services
Sen. R. Edward Houck Virginia Senate	David Hallock Williams, Mullen, Clark and Dobbins
John Stewart Bryan, III Richmond Times Dispatch	Roger C. Wiley Hefty and Wiley
John B. Edwards Smithfield Times	Martika A. Parson Office of the Virginia Attorney General
David E. Anderson McGuire Woods Battle & Booth	Nolan T. Yelich Librarian of Virginia
Frank S. Ferguson Deputy Attorney General	W. Wat Hopkins Virginia Tech

Executive Director:

Maria Everette
(866) 448-4100
meverett@leg.state.va.us
http://dls.state.va.us/foiacouncil.htm

While the FOIA remains cumbersome, the general assembly made a genuine effort to make it more workable when, in 2000, it established the Freedom of Information Advisory Council. The purpose of the twelve-member council is to "encourage and facilitate compliance with the Freedom of Information Act" by issuing advisory opinions, conducting training sessions and publishing educational materials.[4] Maria Everette, an attorney with the Division of Legislative Services, was named executive director of the council. Between

---

[4] Va. Code secs. 2.1-346.2 and 2.1-346.3.

September 2000 and April 2001, she had issued forty-four advisory opinions.[5]

The Virginia Coalition for Open Government also works to ensure open government. The non-profit organization was established in 1996 to enhance the flow of information to citizens in the commonwealth. It monitors access issues and lobbies for increased access to the workings of government.[6]

OFFICIAL RECORDS

The Virginia Freedom of Information Act provides that any citizen of the commonwealth shall be permitted to inspect and copy official records "during the regular office hours of the custodian of such records."[7] Official records are defined as

> all writings and recordings which consist of letters, words or numbers, or their equivalent, set down by handwriting, typewriting, printing, photostatting, photography, magnetic impulse, optical or magneto-optical form, mechanical or electronic recording or other form of data compilation, however stored, and regardless of physical form or characteristics, prepared or owned by, or in the possession of a public body or its officers, employees or agents in the transaction of public business.[8]

The section has been construed to include items as varied as a jail log,[9] mug shots of criminal suspects,[10] and a

---

[5] The council's advisory opinions, and other information, are posted on the council's web page, <http://dls.state.va.us/foiacouncil.htm>.

[6] The web page for the Virginia Coalition for Open Government is <http://opengovva.org/>. The address is Box 2491, Roanoke, VA 24010.

[7] Official records are covered in Va. Code sec. 2.1-342 (1950).

[8] Va. Code sec. 2.1-341 (1950).

[9] 1987-88 Rep. A.G. 37, 1983-84 Rep. A.G. 446, 1980-81 Rep. A.G. 391, 1976-77 Rep. A.G. 250, 1974-75 Rep. A.G. 583. Attorney general's

public school principal's handwritten notes on a person suspected of stealing school property.[11] Medical information on a jail inmate,[12] records of the governor's long-distance telephone calls[13] and tape recordings of 911 emergency telephone calls,[14] on the other hand, lie outside the reach of the act.

Also covered by the act is information held in computer databases maintained by government entities. As of July 1, 1997, every government agency that stored information in computer databases has been required to maintain indexes of documents in those databases. The law also provides that the indexes themselves are official records.

Law Enforcement Documents

Records held by law enforcement agencies have probably caused more controversy in Virginia than any other. The act requires that "criminal incident information relating to felony offenses" must be released. The information may be withheld temporarily, however, if the release is likely to jeopardize an ongoing investigation, jeopardize the safety of an individual, cause a suspect to flee or cause the destruction of evidence.[15] Criminal incident information is defined as general

---

opinions represent an interpretation of the law by the commonwealth's chief law enforcement officer, but they are not binding.

[10] 1990 Rep. A.G. 9. But sec. 2.1-342(B)(1) allows photographs of persons who have been arrested to be withheld if release would jeopardize criminal investigations.

[11] 1983-84 Rep. A.G. 437.

[12] 1987-88 Rep. A.G. 33.

[13] Taylor v. Worrell Enterprises, Inc., 242 Va. 219, 409 S.E.2d 136 (1991).

[14] Tull v. Brown, 255 Va. 177, 494 S.E.2d 855 (1998).

[15] Va. Code sec. 2.1-342.2(B) (1950).

information about criminal activity, including the date and location of the crime, identity of the investigating officer and a description of injuries or property loss.

The act does not provide for the release of criminal incident information regarding misdemeanors, however, and it does not provide for the release of criminal incident reports, those documents used by law enforcement agencies to record incidents under investigation.

In addition, the law allows specific types of records to be withheld:

- complaints, memoranda, correspondence and evidence related to a criminal investigation or prosecution;
- photographs of persons arrested, unless the release of the photograph will not jeopardize the investigation;
- reports submitted in confidence;
- records that would identify anonymous sources;
- records related to neighborhood watch programs;
- records of prison inmates.

The law, therefore, leaves in the hands of law enforcement agencies, considerable discretion as to the types of information to be released and when that information will be released. Since the law does not require access to criminal incident reports, law enforcement agencies can arbitrarily withhold information or can require citizens to see specific officers – the police chief or a public relations officer, for example – who may purposefully be unavailable.

In addition, when disputes arise over whether a document should be released, courts often rule in favor of government agencies. In 1998, for example, the Virginia Supreme Court denied access to a tape recording of a 911 emergency telephone call, even though a transcript of the recording had been made available to the media.[16] The Surry

---

[16] *Tull*, 255 Va. 177, 494 S.E.2d 855 (1998).

County Circuit Court had ruled that the tape was not an official document under the Freedom of Information Act. The Virginia Supreme Court disagreed, holding that the tape recording is an official record, but that it is exempt from disclosure as part of "noncriminal incidents records."[17]

Exemptions

The Freedom of Information Act recognizes that certain documents may be withheld from public view for the sake of privacy or for efficient government operation. In addition to the law enforcement documents described previously, seventy exemptions cover documents containing information relating to topics as varied as fisheries and the Virginia State Lottery.[18] While the law allows certain documents to be withheld from public view, it also allows a custodian of the records to release exempted documents if the release is appropriate. In the following list of exemptions, the numbers in brackets indicate the paragraph number of Virginia Code section 2.1-342.01 in which the exemption is described:

- tax records [2];
- scholastic records [2, 3];
- medical and mental health records [5];
- working papers of members of the general assembly, the governor, the lieutenant governor, the attorney general or any chief executive officer of a political subdivision or state-supported institution of higher education [6];

---

[17] 255 Va. at 183, 494 S.E.2d at 585. Non-criminal incident records are exempt from disclosure under Va. Code sec 15.2-1722 (1950). The incidents are described as "noncriminal occurrences of general interest to law-enforcement agencies" and include missing persons, lost and found reports, suicides and accidental deaths.

[18] Va. Code sec. 2.1-342.01 (1950).

- written opinions of a city or county attorney to the attorney's board [7];
- documents concerning a matter which is properly the subject of a closed session [8, 14];
- letters of recommendation to educational institutions for employment or concerning receipt of an honor [7];
- library records that would identify patrons or materials those patrons borrowed [9];
- tests used by public bodies to evaluate student or employee performance [10];
- various kinds of proprietary or vendor information [16, 18, 19, 22, 61, 66];
- records that would identify persons in rape crisis centers or battered spouse programs [24];
- computer software [25];
- notes involving confidential investigations by a number of agencies, including the Department of Personnel and Training, the Department of Medical Assistance, and the Department of Social Services; investigations under the Human Rights Act; and investigations by the Auditor of Public Accounts and the Joint Legislative Audit and Review Commission [26, 28, 31, 32];
- customer account information of public utilities [30];
- documents related to the Toxic Substances Information Act and hazardous waste facilities [23, 34];
- records about the location and identification of rare, threatened or endangered plants and animals [36];
- records related to the State Lottery Department [37, 38];
- information related to the establishment of new or expansion of existing clinical health services [44];
- information about features of security systems used to control access to or use of automated date processing of telecommunications systems [45];

- business and personnel records of the University of Virginia, the University of Virginia Medical Center and the Medical College of Virginia Hospitals Authority [58, 60].

Often, the exemptions to disclosure are easy to apply. Sometimes, however, courts are called upon to interpret the law to determine whether documents and information should be released. And sometimes those interpretations border on the absurd. In 1996, for example, the Virginia Supreme Court held that the results of a student government elections at a high school constituted scholastic records and, therefore, that a principal was justified in withholding the information.[19] Following elections at Centreville High School in Fairfax County, the editor of the school's student newspaper asked for a complete tally of the votes. The request was denied because, school officials said, the vote totals would embarrass students who did not win seats in the elections. The student sued and, in *Wall v. Fairfax County School Board,* the state supreme court, assuming that the vote total is an official record, said the information could be withheld as scholastic records.[20]

A year later the Virginia Senate adopted a bill amending the FOIA so that information so obviously public could not be withheld by school officials, but the bill did not pass the house of delegates.

The Virginia Supreme Court has also held that the governor was not required under the Freedom of Information Act to release documents revealing long distance telephone calls he had made. A requirement for the governor to release information about such phone calls, the court held, would unreasonably impair his ability to perform his duties as chief executive. The court determined, therefore, that the general

---

[19] Wall v. Fairfax County School Board, 252 Va. 156, 475 S.E.2d 803 (1996).

[20] 252 Va. at 158-59, 475 S.E.2d at 805.

assembly had not intended to require mandatory disclosure of the records.[21]

Procedures for Access

A citizen is not required to state a reason for seeing a specific document; the citizen need only ask to see the document. The citizen, therefore, must know the identity of the custodian of the specific record being sought. The clerk of circuit court, for example, is responsible for the court records; the sheriff is responsible for jail records; the superintendent of schools is responsible for school budgeting documents. And, since the act grants the right of access to citizens, the custodian of the records may legally refuse to produce a record for a person who is not a citizen of the commonwealth unless that person represents a news organization that circulates or broadcasts into the commonwealth.

When a request is made for access to an official document, the custodian, within five working days, must respond by:

- providing the record;
- refusing to provide the record and explaining in writing which of the seventy-one exemptions applies;
- providing the record with certain portions deleted and explaining in writing which exemption applies to the deleted portions; or,
- explaining that the record cannot be provided within the five-day deadline. The agency then has an additional seven days in which to provide the record or explain why it is exempt from the provisions of the act.

Failure to respond to a request for access to an official record is deemed a denial of the record and is a violation of the law.

---

[21] *Taylor,* 242 Va. at 224, 409 S.E.2d at 139-40.

If the request is for an unusually large number of records or if there are other extenuating circumstances, a public agency may petition the court for additional time in which to provide the records requested.

In addition, the agency may charge reasonable fees for search time, computer time and copying. The law specifies, however, that the charges shall not exceed the actual cost to a public body for supplying the records. Indeed, the state attorney general has said it is unreasonable to charge a newspaper for the salary of an employee whose sole task it was to watch a reporter inspect the minutes of a town council meeting.[22] The agency may also seek advance payment if it determines that the cost of producing the record will be more than $200.

Finally, the law specifies that no public agency is required to create or prepare documents for citizens if those documents do not already exist. The purpose of the act is to provide public access to existing documents, not to require agencies to create documents. The provision that an agency not be required to create a document has been enforced even in the face of a violation of the law. In *Hale v. Washington County School Board* the Virginia Supreme Court ruled that a closed session held by the board was invalid, but did not require the board to provide a written summary of the discussion that occurred during that invalid meeting.[23]

PUBLIC MEETINGS

The Virginia Freedom of Information Act provides that all meetings of public bodies, including work sessions in which

---

[22] 1989 Rep. A.G. 12.

[23] 241 Va. 76, 81, 400 S.E.2d 175, 177-78 (1991).

no votes are cast, shall be held in public, and that notice of the time, date and place of the meetings shall be furnished to anyone seeking that information. In addition, the law provides that anyone may photograph, film or record the meetings, but that the public body may adopt rules governing the placement of equipment.[24]

A meeting is defined in the law as any gathering of a quorum or three members of a public body, whichever constitutes fewer people. The law notes, however, that gatherings of two or more members of a public body at a function not intended for the discussion or transaction of public business are not illegal.[25] The Virginia Attorney General has said that social functions do not fall within the purview of the act if there is no evidence that the functions were prearranged with the purpose of discussing or transacting business.[26]

"Public body" is defined as:

> any legislative body, authority, board, bureau, commission, district or agency of the Commonwealth or of any political subdivision of the Commonwealth, including cities, towns and counties; municipal council, governing bodies of counties, school boards and planning commissions; boards of visitors of state institutions of higher education; and other organizations, corporations or agencies in the Commonwealth, supported wholly or principally by public funds.[27]

The definition, therefore, is wide-ranging. It includes committees and subcommittees of public bodies. Indeed, a circuit court judge has held that a meeting of two members of a board of supervisors was a meeting under the law when those

---

[24] Public meetings are covered in Va. Code sec. 2.1-343 (1950).

[25] Va. Code sec. 2.1-343(G) (1950).

[26] 1982-83 Rep. A.G. 721

[27] Va. Code sec. 2.1-341 (1950).

two members constituted the board's finance committee.[28] The state attorney general has also construed the definition to include a student senate meeting at a public university.[29]

The law also prohibits meetings by use of electronic communications unless members of the public are provided with access to the meeting and the ability to hear the business being conducted.[30]

Closed Meetings: Topics for Discussion

The law allows public bodies to hold closed sessions for a variety of reasons, from matters related to the state lottery, to consideration of honorary degrees to matters related to gifts, bequests or grants to the Virginia Museum of Fine Arts or the Science Museum of Virginia.[31]

Closed sessions may be held for the purposes of discussion only; no action may be taken in closed sessions. The law does not require public bodies to discuss matters in closed sessions, but allows such sessions to be held if matters fall within one of twenty-six categories. In the following list of exemptions, the numbers in brackets indicate the paragraph number of Virginia Code section 2.1-344 in which the exemption is described:

- personnel matters, including discussions involving the hiring, firing, discipline, promotion and assignment of

---

[28] Shenandoah Publishing House, Inc. v. Shenandoah County Board of Supervisors, 22 Med. L. Rptr. (BNA) 1177 (Shenandoah Circuit 1993).

[29] 1982-83 Rep. A.G. 440.

[30] Va. Code sec. 2.1-343.1 (1950).

[31] Closed sessions are covered in Va. Code secs. 2.1-344 - 2.1-344.1 (1950). In 2000, the Virginia General Assembly rewrote the Freedom of Information Act, changing the name of that portion of a meeting held outside public fiew from "executive session" to "closed session."

public employees; consideration of the admission or disciplining of students [1, 2];

- discussions necessary to protect the privacy of individuals in personal matters not related to public business [4];
- discussions concerning the acquisition, sale or use of real property; discussions of a prospective business or industry locating within a community, if there has been no previous announcement [3, 5];
- meetings with attorneys to receive legal advice [7];
- discussions of tests or examinations; consideration of honorary degrees or special awards [10, 11];
- discussions of gifts, bequests and fund-raising for state colleges and universities, the Virginia Museum of Fine Arts and the Science Museum of Virginia [8, 9];
- consideration by a house of the general assembly of disciplinary action against a member related to the member's disclosure statement [12];
- discussion by the governor and any economic advisory board reviewing forecasts of economic activity [14];
- discussion of lottery game information and studies [16];
- various information related to local crime commissions, corrections resources boards and the Board of Corrections [17, 18, 19];
- discussion of plans to protect the public safety as it relates to terrorist activity [21].

Closed Meetings: Legal Requirements & Limits

For a closed session to be legal, certain requirements must be met before, during and after the session.

First, a board may go into closed session only upon a majority vote in open session. The specific purpose of the session is to be stated, reasonably identifying the substance of the matters to be discussed, including a specific reference to the section of the act under which the topic falls. The Virginia Supreme Court has ruled that the topic to be discussed must be specifically identified, but that the body is not required to disclose the topic in detail. "To do so," the court ruled, "would tend to defeat the very confidentiality that the exemption safeguards."[32]

Following the closed session, the board must reconvene in open session, and each member of the board must certify "to the best of that member's knowledge" that the board, while in closed session, discussed only matters the law allows to be discussed in such a session and only those matters identified in the motion by which closed session was convened. The certification must take place with a roll call of the members. The law provides that any member of the board who cannot certify is required to indicate "the substance of the departure that, in his judgment, has taken place."

The certification section of the act, which was added in 1989, has caused considerable controversy. Some public officials are offended, claiming that the act presumes that they will attempt to circumvent the law by using closed sessions to discuss any matters they so choose. Indeed, one member of the Montgomery County School Board refused to adhere to the certification requirement, claiming his right not to incriminate himself under the Fifth Amendment to the U.S. Constitution.

Finally, no action taken in closed session is valid. According to the law, any action taken by a public body, even actions on matters discussed in private, must be taken in open session. In addition, all actions must be taken by a public vote – members of public bodies are not allowed to vote on any issues by means of secret ballot.

---

[32] Marsh v. Richmond Newspapers, Inc., 223 Va. 245, 255, 288 S.E.2d 415, 420 (1982).

EVASION AND ENFORCEMENT OF THE LAW

A Freedom of Information Act is only as good as efforts of citizens to enforce it. Over the years public bodies have tried time and again to evade the provisions of the law. Some of these efforts have resulted in amendments to the act.

The Roanoke City School Board, for example, in the early 1980s began holding discussions of school business by means of conference telephone calls. The Virginia Attorney General issued an opinion stating that the calls constituted "meetings" and, therefore, violated the Freedom of Information Act.[33] The state supreme court, however, ruled that the conference calls were not "meetings" for purposes of the act and, therefore, were legal.[34]

The General Assembly responded by amending the act in 1989, specifically outlawing conference calls, unless the times of the calls are announced and access is available for those who want to listen.

The General Assembly, however, has also left a loophole in the law that became apparent in 1991. The law requires public bodies to announce the time and place of informal as well as formal meetings. The General Assembly is exempt from that provision of the act, however. Because of the exemption, Richmond Circuit Judge Randall Johnson ruled that the Senate Finance Committee was not in violation of the law when it held a meeting at a private hunting lodge during the Christmas holidays in 1990.[35] The Virginia chapter of the American Civil Liberties Union brought suit seeking to open such meetings to the public.

---

[33] 1982-83 Rep. A.G. 446.

[34] Roanoke School Board v. Times-World Corp., 226 Va. 185, 207 S.E.2d 256 (1983).

[35] American Civil Liberties Union of Virginia v. Andrews, Case No. HB-342-4 (Richmond Circuit 1991), slip opinion.

Johnson, however, held that the meeting was obviously informal, even though staff members made a presentation and distributed material related to the state budget. Because the meeting was informal, the committee, as part of the general assembly, was not required to give public notice and there was no violation of the act, Johnson ruled.[36] The ACLU decided not to appeal the case because, ACLU attorney David P. Baugh said, the state supreme court would likely affirm Johnson's ruling.[37]

Some public bodies have also used the provision that discussion of legal matters may be discussed in secret to hide certain discussions from the public. The state's attorney general, however, has said that discussions of the law are not automatically exempt from public view. There must be "more than a desire to discuss general legal matters," the attorney general wrote. The statute "requires that there be a specific legal dispute or specific legal inquiry" before the discussion may be held in closed session.[38]

Any person, including a commonwealth's attorney acting in an official capacity, may initiate a legal action against a public body for violating the act. While a pattern of violations may be necessary for a court to take such a suit seriously,[39] the law provides that a single violation of the act is sufficient to warrant penalties upon a board or public official.

A public official violating the act can be fined between $25 and $1,000. In addition, the court can require a public body to pay the legal expenses of the person bringing the action.

---

[36] *Id.* at 10.

[37] Telephone interview, October 29, 1991.

[38] 1986-87 Rep. A.G. 31. *See also* 1982-83 Rep. A.G. 716.

[39] *See, e.g., Marsh,* 223 Va. at 258, 288 S.E.2d at 422.

Chapter 7

PROTECTING SOURCES AND INFORMATION

In its purest form, journalism is simply observation – the gathering of information from a variety of sources and its distribution to people who want and need it. Sometimes the sources of that information need to keep their identities secret, and there is little debate over the proposition that, without the use of confidential sources, many important stories would go untold. There *is* debate, however, over the issue of whether journalists have – or should have – a legal right to refuse to identify sources when asked to do so by law enforcement, or other government, officials. And if they do have such a right, when should it yield to the needs of the government for the information?

The U.S. Supreme Court recognizes the importance to journalists of confidential sources, but has ruled that the First Amendment does not guarantee journalists the right to keep the identities of sources secret.[1] The Court has been clear in its proclamations that journalists have no rights not also enjoyed by non-journalists.[2] Instead, the Court has left it to the states to determine when journalists are protected by a privilege

---

[1] Branzburg v. Hayes, 408 U.S. 665, 690 (1972).

[2] *Id.* at 667. *See also,* Pell v. Procunier, 417 U.S. 817 (1974) and Houchins v. KQED, 438 U.S. 1 (1978), in which the Court refused to grant the press access to government property, in part because access could not also be granted to the public at large.

allowing them to keep sources confidential, or whether the privilege exists at all.[3]

And a number of states have responded. Thirty states and the District of Columbia have passed laws – called "shield laws" – protecting journalists from being forced to reveal their sources unless state governments demonstrate a crucial need for the information.[4] The criteria many states use to balance a journalist's need to keep a source secret with the state's need for the identity of the source is tied to Justice Potter Stewart's dissenting opinion in *Branzburg v. Hayes,* the Supreme Court's landmark case involving confidential sources.[5] In that dissent, Justice Stewart suggested that reporters be required to reveal their confidential sources only if the government clearly demonstrates that:[6]

- there is probable cause to believe the journalist has information clearly relevant to a specific, probable violation of law;
- the information sought cannot be obtained by alternative means less destructive of First Amendment rights;

---

[3] *See, for example,* Winegard v. Oxberger, 258 N.W.2d 847 (Iowa 1977), *cert. denied,* 436 U.S. 905 (1978); State v. Sandstrom, 224 Kan. 573, 581 P.2d 812 (1978), *cert. denied,* 440 U.S. 929 (1979); Maressa v. New Jersey Monthly, 89 N.J. 176, 445 A.2d 376, *cert. denied,* 459 U.S. 907 (1982); and Brown v. Commonwealth, 214 Va. 755, 204 S.E.2d 429, *cert. denied,* 419 U.S. 966 (1974), in which state supreme courts have upheld a qualified privilege of keeping sources and information confidential, and the U.S. Supreme Court has let the state rulings stand by denying *certiorari.*

[4] *Confidential Sources and Information, A Practical Guide for Reporters in the 50 States and D.C., Pull-Out Section,* THE NEWS MEDIA AND THE LAW, Summer 1998, at 3.

[5] Justice Stewart was joined in his dissent by Justices William Brennan and Thurgood Marshall, 408 U.S. at 725.

[6] 408 U.S. at 743 (Stewart, J., dissenting). The majority is sometimes given credit for this three-part test, but the majority in *Branzburg* clearly did not endorse such a test. *See infra* notes 21-24 and accompanying text.

- there is a compelling and overriding interest in the information.

Appellate courts have come to rely on the test by means of a serpentine route. In *Branzburg,* Justice Lewis Powell, who cast the deciding vote supporting the majority's position that the First Amendment does not grant to journalists the right to keep sources confidential, wrote a short concurring opinion noting that efforts by prosecutors to annex the media would not be tolerated. A proper balance should be struck between freedom of the press and the obligation on citizens to testify when called upon, Justice Powell wrote.[7]

Powell provided no guidelines for a test to balance these competing interests, however. He simply wrote that journalists who believed subpoenas were not issued in good faith would have "access to the court on a motion to quash and an appropriate protective order may be entered." These controversies, Justice Powell suggested, would be determined on a case-by-case basis.[8] In the absence of a test from the Court or Justice Powell, then, appellate courts have often turned to Stewart's dissent.

The Virginia General Assembly has passed no shield law, but the commonwealth provides protection for confidential sources and information nevertheless. In *Brown v. Commonwealth,*[9] the Virginia Supreme Court established a

---

[7] *Id.* at 709-10 (Powell, J., concurring).

[8] *Id.* at 710 (Powell, J., concurring). While Justice Powell provided no specific guidelines for a balancing test, courts have not hesitated to use his concurrence as a foundation for denying the privilege of confidentiality. *See, e.g.,* U.S. v. Model Magazine Distributors, Inc., 955 F.2d 229, 233 (4th Cir. 1992). *See also* Phillip Randolph Roach, Jr., *The Newsman's Confidential Source Privilege in Virginia,* 22 U. RICH. L. REV. 377, 386-87 (1988), in which Justice Powell is given credit for a balancing test.

[9] 214 Va. 755, 204 S.E.2d 429, *cert. denied,* 419 U.S. 966 (1974). Virginia was the first state to recognize the privilege of confidentiality through case

qualified privilege that, by intent or not, follows Justice Stewart's guidelines. In *Brown,* the court recognized that

> as a news-gathering mechanism, a newsman's privilege of confidentiality of information and identity of his source is an important catalyst to the free flow of information guaranteed by the freedom of press clause of the First Amendment.[10]

The state court, however, agreed with the U.S. Supreme Court, holding that journalists have no First Amendment right to keep sources and information confidential. Such confidentiality is allowed only by the grant of a privilege by the commonwealth, the court held, and the privilege must yield to overriding governmental interests, such as effective law enforcement. "But," the court noted, "we think the privilege of confidentiality should yield only when the defendant's need is essential to a fair trial," a determination that must be made on a case-by-case basis.[11]

The need for confidential information is essential, the court held, and outweighs the journalist's privilege of confidentiality:[12]

(a) when the information is not available from alternative sources, and

(b) when one of three additional criteria is met:

(i) the material is needed to prove any element of a criminal offense;

(ii) the material is needed to prove a defense asserted by the defendant; or

---

law. Since *Brown,* fifteen states have done so. *Confidential Sources and Information, supra* note 4 at 7-24.

[10] 214 Va. at 757, 204 S.E.2d at 431.

[11] *Id.*

[12] *Id.*

(iii) the material is needed to mitigate the penalty in the alleged crime.

In *Brown,* the court held that the identity of the journalist's source was not essential to the case. The case began when the *Free Lance Star* published a story about a shooting death. Attorneys for the suspect in the murder wanted reporter Helaine Patterson to reveal the sources she used for her published account of the incident. Patterson's story reported details of the shooting that varied from official reports.[13]

The Virginia Supreme Court held that the identity of the source was irrelevant to the case since the inconsistencies were not material and, therefore, did not outweigh the journalist's privilege.[14]

Federal courts in Virginia have extended the privilege to information and sources in civil, as well as criminal, actions. A leading case in the commonwealth is *LaRouche v. National Broadcasting Company.*[15] In that case the Fourth U.S. Circuit Court of Appeals applied what was essentially Stewart's three-part test in allowing NBC to keep confidential sources it used in preparing two broadcasts. Under the test, a journalist could be required to reveal confidential sources or information if it could be shown that (a) the information is clearly relevant, (b) the information can be obtained by no alternative means, (c) there is a compelling interest in the information.[16] The court ruled that Lyndon LaRouche had not exhausted other means of finding the information he was seeking from NBC.[17]

---

[13] 214 Va. at 755-56, 204 S.E.2d at 430.

[14] 214 Va. at 758, 204 S.E.2d at 431.

[15] 780 F.2d 1134 (4th Cir. 1986). *See also* Gilbert v. Allied Chemical Corporation, 411 F. Supp. 505, 510 (E.D. Va. 1976), and Stickels v. General Rental Co., 750 F. Supp. 729 (E.D. Va. 1990)

[16] *Id.* at 1139.

[17] *Id.*

The test has not been applied by a Virginia appellate court. Richmond Circuit Judge T. J. Markow, however, applied it in a controversial case involving Philip Morris and ABC. Judge Markow first required ABC to provide confidential information and reveal the identity of a source to the tobacco company, then later reversed himself and upheld the network's claim of confidentiality. In his first ruling, Judge Markow found that the (a) the information was clearly relevant to Philip Morris's claim that ABC broadcast with actual malice a story alleging that the tobacco company spiked cigarettes with nicotine, (b) that the information was available from no other source, and (c) there was a compelling interest in the information.[18] Three days after he issued his ruling, Judge Markow ordered that it not be enforced and subsequently agreed to a rehearing on the matter.[19] More than six months later, Judge Markow reversed himself and held that Philip Morris needed to show that it had exhausted other "reasonably available sources" without locating the information.[20] Markow allowed ABC to keep the information confidential, and the parties settled the case a month later.

In reversing himself, Judge Markow made what has become a common error. He wrote that, in *Branzburg v. Hayes,* "the Supreme Court described a three part analysis that a court should make before declaring that confidential sources be disclosed."[21] The description of the three-part analysis came in Justice Stewart's dissenting opinion, not in the majority

---

[18] Philip Morris Companies v. American Broadcasting Companies, No. LX-816-3, opinion letter, at 8-10 (Richmond Circuit, January 26, 1995).

[19] *Tobacco Companies Launch Barrage of Subpoenas Seeking Reporters' Records,* THE NEWS MEDIA & THE LAW, Winter 1995, 4.

[20] Philip Morris v. American Broadcasting Companies, Inc., LX-816-3, opinion letter, at 3 (Richmond Circuit, July 11, 1995).

[21] *Id.*

opinion.[22]   The majority in *Branzburg* refused to grant to journalists a privilege not also enjoyed by other citizens[23] and, in doing so, had some harsh language for the claim that journalists deserved such a privilege.[24]

What is unclear is whether the *LaRouche* test may supplant the *Brown* test in Virginia. It probably won't make a difference. The differences between the two tests are primarily semantic. Both are based in large part on Justice Stewart's dissent and both require disclosure when material is shown to be essential and when it is unavailable from alternative sources.

Another important point, however, is that courts in Virginia have not been willing to extend the privilege to non-confidential sources. The U.S. District Court for the Eastern District of Virginia, in one case, required journalists to turn over files containing secondary materials gathered as part of their research,[25] and, in a second, required a newspaper to produce unpublished photographs taken at an accident scene.[26] The basis for the rulings was that, while a privilege exists for a journalist to withhold confidential information, the privilege does not extend to material for which the journalist has not guaranteed confidentiality to a source.

---

[22] *See supra* note 5-7 and accompanying text.

[23] 408 U.S. at 690.

[24] *Id.* at 691-708.

[25] *Gilbert,* 411 F. Supp. at 511.

[26] *Stickels,* 750 F. Supp. at 732.

Confidential Sources Tests		
Stewart Test	**Virginia Test**	**LaRouche Test**
There is probable cause to believe the journalist has information clearly relevant to a specific, probable violation of the law.		The information is clearly relevant
The information sought cannot be obtained by alternative means less destructive of First Amendment rights.	The information being sought is not available from alternative sources.	The information cannot be obtained by alternative means.
There is a compelling and overriding interest in the information.	The material being sought is needed to prove any element of a criminal offense, or The material is needed to prove a defense asserted by the defendant, or The material is needed to mitigate the penalty in the alleged crime.	There is a compelling interest for the information.

Oddly enough, in this second case, the newspaper had voluntarily allowed the defendant in a lawsuit to examine the photographs to determine whether they might be of value. After examining the photographs, the defendant continued its effort to require the newspaper to provide the photographs for use in court. That continued effort, the court ruled, demonstrated that the photographs were important to the case.[27]

---

[27] *Id.*

The Virginia Supreme Court has not been asked to rule on attempts to gain access to unpublished notes, photographs and other materials that are not confidential. Such a ruling would be important since requests for unpublished materials are more frequent than requests for the identities of confidential sources. Because of the rulings from the federal district court, however, judges in the commonwealth can be expected to require journalists to provide non-confidential, unpublished materials.

One other point needs to be made.

Journalists should be clear when they discuss with sources the possibility of keeping identities or information confidential. This has become increasingly important because of the U.S. Supreme Court's ruling in *Cohen v. Cowles Media, Inc.* in 1991.[28] In that case, the Court allowed damages to be assessed against a newspaper because the newspaper breached a promise of confidentiality. Reporters for the newspaper had promised confidentiality to a campaign worker in exchange for information about a candidate. Editors for the paper, however, decided that the more important story was that the campaign worker provided information to smear a candidate and ordered his name published over the objections of the reporters.

Journalists should also avoid promising confidentiality to sources without discussing the ramifications of the promise with editors or news directors and learning the policy of their news organizations. Some news organizations, for example, require journalists to be willing to reveal the identities of sources to their supervisors before stories based on those sources will be published or broadcast.

Finally, journalists should be clear on what actions to take, questions to ask and responses to give when they receive

---

[28] 501 U.S. 663 (1991).

requests for information and, more importantly, when they receive subpoenas demanding information or materials.

Chapter 8

COVERING COURTS IN VIRGINIA

The conflict between the Sixth Amendment right to a fair trial and the First Amendment right of a free press, the U.S. Supreme Court has noted, is "almost as old as the Republic."[1] These two rights are basic to a democratic society and are implicitly related: The Sixth Amendment provides that a person shall be treated fairly by the criminal justice system; the First Amendment ensures that the courts shall be open to public scrutiny so citizens can determine whether justice is being fulfilled. The conflict, as one Virginia scholar has noted, "is not a clash between right and wrong, but between right and right. It is not a conflict between hero and villain, but between two heroes," making the issue very difficult to resolve.[2]

Traditionally, when First and Sixth Amendment rights have come into conflict, the parties involved have attempted to resolve their differences by taking one of two paths: adjudication in the courts or voluntary guidelines for covering trials and hearings.

Both paths have been taken in Virginia.

---

[1] Nebraska Press Association v. Stuart, 427 U.S. 539, 547 (1976).

[2] Sam G. Riley, The Free Press-Fair Trial Controversy: A Discussion of the Issues Involved and an Examination of Pre-Trial Publicity by Survey Research, unpublished doctoral dissertation, University of North Carolina at Chapel Hill, 1970. Dr. Riley is professor of communication studies at Virginia Tech.

COURT-ESTABLISHED GUIDELINES

Trial judges in Virginia have considerable authority over conduct in their courtrooms. That authority includes the power to punish a person for critical remarks aimed at the judge, the power to exclude from the court any person the judge believes may be disruptive and the power to change the location of a trial because of pre-trial publicity.

Contempt of Court

A judge's power to punish a person for contempt of court extends to punishment for any "vile, contemptuous or insulting language addressed to or published of a judge for or in respect of any act or proceeding."[3]

The Virginia Supreme Court has held that judges are not free from criticism, but when the critical remarks tend to destroy respect for the courts, the critic may be held in contempt.[4] The statute has rarely been invoked.

Closed Hearings & Trials

Judges have been less hesitant in using a statute that allows them to close proceedings. State law provides that:

> In the trial of all criminal cases, whether the same be felony or misdemeanor cases, the court may, in its discretion, exclude from the trial any persons whose presence would impair the conduct of a fair trial, provided that the right of the accused to a public trial shall not be violated.[5]

---

[3] Va. Code sec. 18.2-456 (1950).

[4] Weston v. Commonwealth, 195 Va. 175, 183-84, 77 S.E.2d 405, 409-10 (1953).

[5] Va. Code sec. 19.2-266 (1950).

Using this statute as a basis, judges have not hesitated to exclude the press from courtrooms, sometimes indiscriminately. They have done so, even though the U.S. Supreme Court, using a Virginia case as its vehicle, has established that trials may be closed only in rare circumstances. In *Richmond Newspapers, Inc. v. Virginia,* the court held that trials are to be open unless there is some overriding government interest that mandates closure.[6] And, the Court said, such an interest must be clearly articulated in writing by the trial judge.[7]

In 1981 the Virginia Supreme Court, following the precepts of *Richmond Newspapers,* established a series of guidelines to help trial courts resolve conflicts involving access to criminal proceedings. The case, *Richmond Newspapers, Inc. v. Commonwealth,*[8] is often called *Richmond Newspapers II* to distinguish it from the earlier case involving the same newspaper company.[9]

Richmond Newspapers II consolidated three murder cases in which trial judges had summarily closed pretrial proceedings to the public and press.[10] The Virginia Supreme Court ruled that hearings in Virginia are presumed to be open and that none of the hearings should have been closed.[11] Unlike

---

[6] 448 U.S. 555, 564-575 (1980).

[7] *Id.* at 581.

[8] 222 Va. 574, 281 S.E.2d 915 (1981).

[9] At the state level, Richmond Newspapers, Inc. v. Virginia was also identified as Richmond Newspapers, Inc. v. Commonwealth. *"Richmond Newspapers I"* and *"Richmond Newspapers II,"* therefore, are used to distinguish the two cases.

[10] 222 Va. at 579, 281 S.E.2d at 917, note 1.

[11] 222 Va. at 592, 281 S.E.2d at 925.

Richmond Newspapers I, the second case never reached the U.S. Supreme Court.[12]

The Virginia Supreme Court began its opinion in *Richmond Newspapers II* by noting that Virginians are guaranteed fair trials by both the Sixth Amendment of the federal Constitution and Article I, Section 8 of the Virginia Constitution.[13] But, the court noted, "A necessary adjunct to a fair trial is an open trial. The presence of the public will ensure that an accused's rights are not denied."[14] Openness, the court held, may improve the quality of testimony, encourage unknown witnesses to come forward with relevant information and cause participants to perform their duties more conscientiously.[15]

While adverse publicity can affect the fairness of trial proceedings, access to pretrial hearings is as important as access to trials, the court noted.[16] Such hearings are often the only adversary proceedings for an accused, and the public has the right to determine for itself whether the proper balance is struck between preventing misconduct on the part of the judicial system and the possibility that a guilty person may go free.[17]

---

[12] *Richmond Newspapers II* involved pretrial hearings, but the guidelines established by the court are based on *Richmond Newspapers I,* and much of the language of the opinion relates to trials. The guidelines, therefore, apparently apply to the closing of trials as well as pretrial hearings. Indeed, the Virginia Court of Appeals applied the guidelines to the closure of trials in the case In re Times-World Corp., 7 Va. App. 317, 373 S.E.2d 474 (Va. Ct. App. 1988).

[13] Both the Sixth Amendment to the U.S. Constitution and the Virginia Constitution provide that a defendant have a speedy and public trial, be informed of the nature of the charges, be allowed to confront witnesses and be allowed to produce evidence.

[14] 222 Va. at 584, 281 S.E.2d at 920.

[15] 222 Va. at 585, 281 S.E.2d at 921.

[16] 222 Va. at 587, 281 S.E.2d at 922.

[17] *Id.*

"To allow the public to view the trial without any knowledge of what has taken place previously," the court held, "would make the right of access a hollow one."[18]

Therefore, the court ruled, absent "an overriding interest articulated in the findings," pretrial hearings, like trials, shall be open to the public, a rule mandated by the Virginia Constitution.[19]

The language used by the state high court came from the U.S. Supreme Court's opinion in *Richmond Newspapers I*. The state court noted, however, that the earlier case did not establish a test for determining what might be a "overriding interest." The court, therefore, adopted the rule that hearings would be open unless the information released in those hearings, which would not otherwise reach jurors, would jeopardize the defendant's right to a fair trial. In addition, the state court held a trial judge should consider alternative measures before closing a hearing and, if closure is required, should only close that portion of the hearing in which the prejudicial information would be introduced.[20]

The court also held that, before a hearing is closed, members of the public should have the opportunity to object. The court, therefore, established procedures trial courts should follow:[21]

- Motions to close hearings should be made in writing and filed with the court before the day of the hearing; the public must be given reasonable notice that a closure hearing will be conducted.

---

[18] 222 Va. at 588, 281 S.E.2d at 922.

[19] *Id*

[20] 222 Va. at 589, 281 S.E.2d at 923.

[21] 222 Va. at 590, 281 S.E.2d at 924.

- The burden is on the party seeking closure to show that an open hearing would jeopardize the defendant's right to a fair trial.
- The party objecting to closure has the burden of showing that reasonable alternatives to closure are available.
- The judge must write an opinion explaining his findings and, if allowing closure, explaining why the alternative measures would not work.
- The judge may receive information outside the hearing of public and the jury to determine whether its release would be prejudicial.

In addition, the Virginia Court of Appeals established a two-part test trial judges should use to determine whether a First Amendment right of access to a hearing or trial is available to the press and public. A trial judge, the court held, must determine (1) whether the judicial event or its process has historically been open and (2) whether public access plays a significant, positive role in the functioning of the process in question.[22] Using the test, the court of appeals ruled that one trial judge erroneously closed jury *voir dire* in a criminal case,[23] and that another trial judge erroneously closed a competency hearing for a murder suspect.[24] The court also held, however, that because the purpose of a discovery hearing has traditionally been to prepare for trial, documents subpoenaed and used in

---

[22] *See, e.g.,* In Re Times-World Corporation, 7 Va. App 317, 324-26, 373 S.E.2d 474, 477-79 (1988); In re Worrell Enterprises, Inc., 14 Va. App. 671, 676, 419 S.E.2d 271, 274 (1992); In re Times-World Corporation, 25 Va. App. 405, 413, 488 S.E.2d 677, 681 (1997). The test was taken from the U.S. Supreme Court case of Press-Enterprise Co. v. Superior Court, 478 U.S. 1, 8 (1986).

[23] In Re Times-World Corporation, 7 Va. App 317, 373 S.E.2d 474 (1988).

[24] In re Times-World Corporation, 25 Va. App. 405, 488 S.E.2d 677 (1997).

such a hearing were not judicial records subject to a right of access.[25]

Not all the state supreme court's rulings have favored openness. In a disturbing opinion handed down in April 2000, the court, by a 4-3 vote, affirmed the closure of preliminary hearings in murder trial and a sexual assault trial because attorneys for the media used a legal remedy the court found to be inappropriate.[26] Attorneys used a writ of mandamus in an effort to compel the judges in the cases to keep open the preliminary hearings. They did so after the judges refused to delay closure in order to hear objections from attorneys for the media. The state supreme court held that mandamus "is an extraordinary remedy" that should be used only in urgent circumstances, and it was inappropriate.[27] Justice Lawrence L. Koontz, joined by Justices Elizabeth B. Lacy and Cynthia D. Kinser, dissented. Justice Koontz wrote that the trial court did not give sufficient consideration to the First Amendment access rights of the media and that "the right of access of the news media to court proceedings is a hollow one without an effective remedy when that right is wrongfully decided."[28] Koontz would have granted the writ.

In addition, the Virginia Supreme Court has held that there is a presumption that civil trials and records will be open, unless there is "an interest so compelling that it cannot be protected reasonably by some measure" other than closure.[29]

---

[25] In re Worrell Enterprises, Inc., 14 Va. App. 671, 419 S.E.2d 271 (1992).

[26] Hertz v. Times-World Corp., 259 Va. 599, 528 S.E.2d 458 (2000).

[27] *Hertz*, 259 Va. at 608-09, 419 S.E.2d at 462-63

[28] 259 Va. at 613, 419 S.E.2d at 466 (Koontz, J., dissenting).

[29] Shenandoah Publishing House, Inc. v. Fanning, 235 Va. 253, 258-59, 368 S.E.2d 253, 256 (1988).

Pre-trial Publicity & Change of Venue

One method of helping ensure that a defendant receives a fair trial in the face of overwhelming publicity, the U.S. Supreme Court has noted, is to change the venue, that is, to move the trial to a location where the publicity has not been as great.[30]

Changes of venue, however, cause many problems. Attorneys, witnesses and other trial participants must physically relocate for the duration of the trial, causing added expense and inconvenience. In addition, the U.S. Constitution provides that a person be tried in the "district wherein the crime shall have been committed."[31] Judges, therefore, do not like to change the venue unless absolutely necessary.

That has been particularly true in Virginia. The Virginia Supreme Court has held that the law presumes that a defendant will get a fair trial from the citizens of the city or county where the crime was committed. This presumption, the court held, must be overcome by a clear showing of widespread prejudice against the defendant.[32]

It is insufficient, the court held, that jurors know about the crime because of publicity. Indeed, even a large amount of publicity about a case or defendant, standing alone, is

---

[30] *See, e.g.,* Rideau v. Louisiana, 373 U.S. 723 (1963), *and* Sheppard v. Maxwell, 384 U.S. 333 (1966).

[31] U.S. Constitution amend. 6.

[32] Coppola v. Commonwealth, 220 Va. 243, 248, 257 S.E.2d 797, 801 (1972), *cert. denied,* 444 U.S. 1103 (1980). *See also,* Stockton v. Commonwealth, 227 Va. 124, 137, 314 S.E.2d 371, 380 (1984), *cert. denied,* 469 U.S. 873 (1984); Pope v. Commonwealth, 234 Va. 114, 120, 360 S.E.2d 352, 356 (1987), *cert. denied,* 485 U.S. 1015 (1988); Gray v. Commonwealth, 233 Va. 313, 333, 356 S.E.2d 157, 168 (1987), *cert. denied,* 484 U.S. 873 (1987); Asher v. Commonwealth, 12 Va. App. 1105, 1113, 408 S.E.2d 906, 911 (1991), *cert. denied,* 506 U.S. 865 (1992).

insufficient cause for a change of venue.[33]   This seems to be particularly true when the reporting on the case is neither inaccurate nor intemperate.[34]

VOLUNTARY GUIDELINES

A number of states have adopted guidelines suggesting the types of information about crimes or criminal suspects that should or should not be released.[35]   There have been rare cases in which courts have required journalists to adhere to these voluntary bench-bar-press guidelines.[36]   The U.S. Supreme Court has made it clear, however, that such gag orders on the press are unconstitutional,[37] even though trial judges may place gag orders on participants in a trial.   Judges sometimes use bench-bar-press guidelines in structuring those gag orders.

Virginia's "Guidelines on Release of Information to the News Media," like those of most states, are based on the American Bar Association Standards on Fair Trial and Free Press, adopted by the ABA House of Delegates in 1966 and revised in 1980.   The guidelines apply to all employees of the Virginia Judicial System and to all circuit court clerks and their employees.

---

[33] Briley v. Commonwealth, 221 Va. 532, 538, 273 S.E.2d 48, 52 (1980), *cert. denied,* 451 U.S. 1031 (1981).

[34] *Id.   See also Stockton,* 227 Va. at 137, 314 S.E.2d at 380.

[35] Good discussions of voluntary guidelines appear in Ruth Walden, *Access to Courts,* in COMMUNICATION AND THE LAW 336-37 (1998); KENT R. MIDDLETON and BILL F. CHAMBERLIN, THE LAW OF PUBLIC COMMUNICATION 4th ed. 418-21 (1997); and WAYNE OVERBECK, MAJOR PRINCIPLES OF MEDIA LAW 1991 Edition 261-63 (1996).

[36] *See, e.g.,* Federated Publications v. Swedberg, 96 Wash. 2d 13, 633 P.2d 74 (1981), *cert. denied,* 456 U.S. 984 (1982).

[37] *See, e.g., Nebraska Press Association,* 427 U.S. at 570.

The Virginia guidelines identify as "releasable" the following information:

- Factual background information about an accused, including name, age, address, employment and family status.
- The substance or text of the charge.
- The fact that the accused denies the charge, if appropriate.
- Any action taken by a judge in open court.
- Anything in official records which have not been sealed by a judge.

The following types of information are identified as "unreleasable":

- Statements about the character or reputation of the accused.
- The contents of any statements by the accused, except a denial of the charges, including possible alibis, admissions or confessions, or the refusal of the accused to make a statement.
- The results of any tests or the refusal of the accused to participate in any tests.
- Statements about the character, reputation or credibility of any prospective witnesses or statements about the anticipated testimony of any witnesses.
- The possibility of a guilty plea or plea bargain.
- Opinions concerning the evidence or arguments in the case, including statements about what evidence may or may not be used.
- Prior criminal records, except as part of the release of public documents.

ELECTRONIC COVERAGE OF TRIALS AND HEARINGS

Ironically, the same section of the Code of Virginia which has allowed judges to exclude the press and public from courtrooms now allows journalists to photograph or electronically record those proceedings. As of July 1, 1992, cameras and tape recorders have been allowed in courtrooms in the commonwealth, with certain restrictions.

The first effort to win approval for cameras in Virginia courtrooms came in the 1970s, but it wasn't until 1987 that the general assembly amended a ban on photographic equipment in the courtrooms to provide for a two-year experiment.[38] The experiment allowed electronic coverage of the Virginia Supreme Court, the Virginia Court of Appeals, two circuit courts and two district courts. The experiment was expanded to include an additional circuit court.[39]

Then, in February 1992, despite two scathing denunciations of the experiment by the Virginia Supreme Court,[40] the general assembly adopted a bill allowing photographic coverage of all courts in the commonwealth.[41]

The coverage is neither absolute nor automatic, however.

A trial judge, for example, has the power under the law to prohibit or interrupt photographic coverage of a trial or to restrict coverage "as he deems appropriate to meet the ends of justice." The law also specifies that the judge must inform the parties in a case of the possibility that the trial will be

---

[38] A good history of Virginia's experience with cameras in courtrooms is in Teresa Keller, Cameras in Courtrooms: An Analysis of Television Court Coverage in Virginia, unpublished doctoral dissertation, University of Tennessee, Knoxville, 1992. Dr. Keller is associate professor of mass communications at Emory and Henry College.

[39] In 1987 photography was allowed in the circuit courts in Bedford County and Virginia Beach and the district courts in Caroline County and Charlottesville. Later, the circuit court in Henrico County was added to the experiment.

[40] The reports were issued to Gov. Charles Robb in 1987 and Gov. Douglas Wilder in 1992.

[41] Senate Bill 480 amended Va. Code sec. 19.2-266 (1950).

photographed by media representatives and allow them to object. An objection by a party does not require a judge to prohibit electronic coverage of a trial or hearing. Such an objection would be considered, among other factors, by the presiding judge.

The law prohibits photographic coverage of proceedings involving adoptions, juveniles, child custody, divorces, spousal support, sexual offenses, motions to suppress evidence and trade secrets. In addition, jurors, police informants, minors, undercover agents, victims of sexual offenses and families of victims of sexual offenses may not be photographed. Finally, there may be no photographic or sound coverage of any conferences involving attorneys or the judge, or any conferences held at the judge's bench or in the judge's chambers.

The law also places restrictions on electronic equipment and media personnel necessary to operate that equipment. It specifies that equipment not be intrusive or distracting. No artificial lights are allowed, and neither cameras nor audio equipment may make distracting sounds. Microphones and wiring for audio equipment must be located in positions approved in advance by the presiding judge. Audio equipment is only allowed if the existing audio system is not suitable for broadcasting.

In addition, the law provides that no more than two television cameras with appropriate personnel; one still photographer with no more than two cameras, each having no more than two lenses, and no more than one audio system are permitted in any courtroom at any one time. As a result, media personnel must pool resources. And, the law states, the media must work out any pooling arrangements "without calling upon the presiding judge to mediate any dispute."

Media representatives are not prohibited from talking with presiding judges. Indeed, the law provides that the Virginia Association of Broadcasters and the Virginia Press

Association designate one television journalist, one radio broadcaster and one still photographer to act as representatives of the media in making pooling arrangements and speaking with presiding judges about the coverage of any proceedings, including the location of equipment within courtrooms.

The law prohibits media personnel from entering or leaving courtrooms, except during recesses, once proceedings begin and prohibits the movement of equipment in or out, without the judge's permission, except prior to or at the end of the proceedings or during the luncheon recess.

In June 1992 the Virginia Association of Broadcasters and the Virginia Press Association responded to the law with a memorandum circulated to their members listing "Courtroom Electronic Journalism Procedures Effective July 1, 1992." The procedures note that "a high degree of cooperation and coordination" will be required between "news agencies that are far more familiar with competition." Specifically, the procedures require that:

- Media organizations require any person assigned to cover a trial proceeding to read the statute and to be briefed on the courtroom procedures.
- Organizations ask the proceeding judge in a specific case to allow electronic coverage of the proceedings in the case.
- Multiple requests to cover a particular case be referred to an area coordinator so pooling arrangements can be developed. The Associated Press and United Press International will be asked to run advisories over the state wire so other media can participate.

The guidelines establish dress codes for media personnel covering trials and procedures for the use of pool equipment. And they identify official media representatives across the state.

Chapter 8: Covering Courts in Virginia

Chapter 9

ADVERTISING REGULATION

Advertising – commercial speech – is protected by both the First Amendment to the U.S. Constitution and the Virginia Constitution – but that protection is limited.

Commercial speech, the U.S. Supreme Court has said, is different from other forms of protected speech, because advertisers can easily evaluate "the accuracy of their messages and the lawfulness of the underlying activity," and because "commercial speech, the offspring of economic self-interest, is a hardy breed of expression that is not 'particularly susceptible to being crushed by overbroad regulation.'"[1] Because of these differences, and to protect consumers from deception, the Supreme Court has allowed greater regulation of commercial speech.[2]

Virginia has taken advantage of the Court's flexibility in this area of mass communication law and has implemented a wide variety of regulations on advertising.

---

[1]Central Hudson Gas & Electric Corp. v. Public Service Commission of New York, 447 U.S. 557, 564, note 6 (1980).

[2] *Id.* at 578.

TRUTH IN ADVERTISING

Virginia law regulating commercial speech is wide-ranging. The commonwealth prohibits the use of false, deceptive or misleading advertisements in general – the prohibition is against any false or deceptive advertising about "anything offered" by a company, organization or individual.[3] The criminal statute is part of Virginia's anti-fraud provisions, however, and has been held only to apply to written advertisements.[4]

State law doesn't stop with this broad prohibition, however. It also prohibits deceptive advertising in a variety of specific areas, including food and restaurants,[5] dentistry,[6] the health professions,[7] insurance policies and insurance company trade practices,[8] automobiles[9] and the source of any sales merchandise.[10]

Similarly, the advertising of certain merchandise – obscene materials,[11] drug paraphernalia,[12] illegal alcohol[13] and electronic eavesdropping equipment,[14] for example – is prohibited, and the advertising of other products is regulated.

In addition, state law strictly regulates the use of some common advertising terms and descriptors. For example, the

---

[3] Va. Code sec. 18.2-216 (1950).

[4] Henry v. R.K. Chevrolet, Inc., 219 Va. 1011, 254 S.E.2d 66 (1979).

[5] Va. Code secs. 3.1-386 - 3.1-401 (1950).

[6] Va. Code sec. 54.1-2706 (1950).

[7] Va. Code sec. 54.1-2403 (1950).

[8] Va. Code secs. 38.2-502 and 38.2-503 (1950).

[9] Va. Code sec. 46.2-1581 (1950).

[10] Va. Code sec. 18.2-222 (1950).

[11] Va. Code sec. 18.2-376 (1950).

[12] Va. Code sec. 18.2-255.1 (1950).

[13] Va. Code sec. 4.1-320 (1950).

[14] Va. Code sec. 19.2-63 (1950).

terms "secondhand," "irregular,"[15] "wholesale,"[16] "going out of business,"[17] "sterling,"[18] "coin silver,"[19] "market value," "suggested retail price," "manufacturer's suggested price," "list price" and similar terms[20] must be used accurately, under penalty of law. The term "official tourist information" can only be used to refer to information disseminated by the commonwealth without charge.[21] And only genuine Smithfield hams – hams cured by the long-cure, dry salt method, aged for six months and processed within the city limits of Smithfield – may be advertised as "Smithfield hams."[22]

ADVERTISING TECHNIQUES AND METHODS

Virginia also regulates a variety of advertising techniques and methods, ranging from bait-and-switch tactics to comparison advertising. Most of the regulations apply to businesses and organizations, rather than to individuals, and few of them apply directly to the mass media. They are important, however, because they affect the types of messages that may or may not be communicated to potential consumers. The law also prohibits the use of a person's name or likeness in an advertisement without permission or, if the person is dead,

---

[15] Va. Code sec. 18.2-218 (1950).

[16] Va. Code sec. 18.2-220 (1950).

[17] Va. Code sec. 18.2-223 (1950).

[18] Va. Code sec. 18.2-233 (1950).

[19] Va. Code sec. 18.2-234 (1950).

[20] Va. Code sec. 59.1-207.4 (1950).

[21] Va. Code sec. 18.2-211 (1950).

[22] Va. Code secs. 3.1-867 and 3.1-868 (1950).

without permission of survivors.[23]   Finally, the commonwealth also regulates political advertising.

Commercial Advertising

Virginia law requires businesses to be able to substantiate any price comparisons they make – whether those comparisons are to goods and services previously provided by the businesses or to goods and services offered by competitors. Specifically, businesses offering goods or services at sales prices must also be able to show that a substantial number of sales were made at the higher prices.[24]   And businesses making comparisons to competitors must be able to show that the comparison is in fact to the competitor's prices for "substantially the same kind and quality" of goods and services.[25]

Auto dealers come under what may be the strictest regulatory scheme in state law. Two pages of the Virginia Code regulate language used to advertise both new and used cars. Regulations cover the use of a variety of terms, including "new," "sticker price," "at cost," "manufacturer's factory invoice" and "free."[26]

Most of the regulations apply strictly to automobile dealers, but individuals are required to accurately report the make, year, model and options available on cars they are selling.[27]

Virginia law also requires that pay-per-service telephone operations – 900 numbers that are commonly advertised by

---

[23] Va. Code sec. 18.2-216.1 (1950). This statute is discussed in greater detail in Chapter 5.

[24] Va. Code sec. 59.1-207.41 (1950).

[25] Va. Code sec. 59.1-207.42 (1950).

[26] Va. Code sec. 46.2-1581 (1950).

[27] Va. Code sec. 18.2-221 (1950).

television stations – must meet specific guidelines. Advertising of pay-per-service operations must include the per-minute cost of each call, along with the average length a call takes in order to benefit from the service. In addition, at the beginning of each call, the caller must be told the rate being charged.[28] And the law prohibits solicitation calls that do not disengage when the receiver of the call hangs up the telephone.[29]

Finally, the law prohibits bait-and-switch tactics. The failure of a business to provide goods or services at advertised prices, the law says, is evidence of false or misleading advertising.[30]

As previously indicated, most advertising regulation applies to advertisers – that is, to the businesses, organizations or individuals selling goods and services – rather than to the mass media. Indeed, the law provides protection for radio and television stations, newspapers and other media organizations that unknowingly publish false or misleading advertising. A publisher of false advertising cannot be found guilty under state law if the publication was based upon copy of information provided by an advertiser or by the provider of goods and services.[31]

Media organizations, therefore, are under no obligation to verify all the information in potential advertisements – whether display or classified – before publishing those advertisements. Only when the copy of an advertisement is obviously suspect, does a media organization become liable for its publication.

---

[28] Va. Code sec. 59.1-430 (1950).

[29] Va. Code sec. 18.2-425.1 (1950).

[30] Va. Code sec. 18.2-217 (1950).

[31] Va. Code sec. 3.1-390 (1950).

In addition, the law provides that honest mistakes cannot be the basis of a false advertising claim,[32] so advertisers themselves are not liable when advertisements are false, if the advertisements were written and published in good faith. There are exceptions to this rule, however.[33]

Political Advertising

Virginia law requires campaign literature to bear the name and affiliation of the author of the literature or, if the literature is disseminated by a person not affiliated with an organization, the person's address.[34] The law is probably unconstitutional, despite an attorney general's opinion to the contrary.

The U.S. Supreme Court struck down a similar law in 1995.[35] Almost immediately, M. Bruce Meadows, secretary of the Virginia Board of Elections, sought an attorney general's opinion as to how the Court's ruling would apply to Virginia law. Then Attorney General James S. Gilmore responded that the portion of Virginia law prohibiting anonymous campaign literature related to ballot issues probably *is not* constitutional, but that portion of the law prohibiting anonymous campaign literature related to candidates for public office probably *is* constitutional.[36]   Gilmore went through a protracted examination of the law and determined that the state's interest in identifying speakers in a political campaign outweighed the desire of those speakers to remain anonymous. What Gilmore ignored was the fact that the same arguments would also apply

---

[32] Va. Code sec. 18.2-243 (1950).

[33] *See* discussion accompanying *infra* notes 46-50.

[34] Va. Code 24.2-1014 (1950).

[35] McIntyre v. Ohio Elections Commission, 514 U.S. 334 (1995).

[36] 1995 Rep. Atty. Gen. 170.

to ballot issues, yet the Court had ruled such provisions unconstitutional.

LEGAL ADVERTISING

Legal advertising is a special area of the law that relates directly to newspapers. The law requires that certain actions by local governments be made public through local newspapers. Since the U.S. Supreme Court has ruled that the government cannot force such a publication upon newspapers,[37] local governments are required to buy advertising to publicize these legal actions.

Local governments often have a significant amount of legal advertising, some of which must be published weekly for four consecutive weeks.[38] The account for a county's legal advertising, therefore, can be quite lucrative.

Until 1992, legal advertisements could only be published in local newspapers that had histories of continuous publication, lists of paying subscribers and second-class mailing permits.[39] An amendment to the law that year, however, made it possible for free-circulation newspapers to be designated as outlets for legal advertising. Free-circulation newspapers often have no second-class mailing permits because the bulk of their distribution is through newsstands, newsracks or unsolicited home delivery.

Under the law, a newspaper may petition a circuit court and may receive authority to publish legal advertising for up to a year if the newspaper has been published in the community for at least a year, employs a full-time news staff and reports

---

[37] Miami Herald v. Tornillo, 418 U.S. 241 (1974).

[38] Va. Code sec. 8.01-323 (1950).

[39] Va. Code sec. 8.01-324 (1950.).

local current events, has an editorial page, accepts letters to the editor and has an audit of circulation certified by an independent auditing firm.[40]

ADVERTISING AND THE COURTS

In the few advertising cases that have reached Virginia appellate courts, the courts have affirmed the government's right to regulate commercial speech,[41] but have not allowed blanket regulations.

In *Adams Outdoor Advertising v. Newport News,* for example, the Virginia Supreme Court struck down a city ordinance that regulated billboards.[42] The ordinance allowed on-site business signs that advertised services or products, but prohibited such signs off-site and also prohibited non-commercial on-site signs.[43] The court ruled that the ordinance discriminated against non-commercial advertising and held that it was unconstitutional.[44] Similarly, the Fourth U.S. Circuit Court of Appeals, in a Virginia case, found unconstitutional an Arlington County ordinance limiting the number of signs that could be posted on private, residential property.[45]

In what may be the Virginia Supreme Court's most significant ruling involving advertising, the court held that a published newspaper advertisement was tantamount to a binding contract, even if the advertisement contained a

---

[40] *Id.*

[41] *See, e.g.,* Dotti v. Virginia Board of Medicine, 12 Va. App. 735, 407 S.E.2d 8 (1991).

[42] 236 Va. 370, 373 S.E.2d 917 (1988).

[43] 236 Va. at 372-79, 373 S.E.2d at 918-21.

[44] 236 Va. at 388, 373 S.E.2d at 926-27.

[45] Arlington County Republican Committee v. Arlington County, 983 F.2d 587 (4th Cir. 1993).

typographical error. The case was *Chang v. First Colonial Savings Bank* and was based on a very narrow set of facts.[46]

The case began when Chia T. Chang and Shin S. Chang read a newspaper advertisement for a savings program offered by First Colonial Savings Bank. According to the advertisement, a depositor would receive a free color television set upon depositing $14,000 into a savings account that matured in three and one-half years. Upon maturity, according to the ad, the account would pay $20,136.12.

The Changs opened an account and received their television set, but three and one-half years later they were told that the ad contained a typographical error. It should have required a deposit of $15,000 rather than $14,000. They were also told that because they did not deposit $15,000, they would receive $18,823.93 instead of the higher figure.[47]

The Changs argued that the newspaper advertisement constituted an offer, which they accepted, establishing a contract under the law. The bank argued that the advertisement did not constitute an offer, but constituted an invitation to make an offer to the general public, and that the Changs merely responded to the invitation.[48]

The court noted that newspaper advertisements are not generally considered offers under the law, "but merely invitations to bargain." The court noted a very narrow and limited exception to the rule, however: "Where the offer is clear, definite, and explicit, and leaves nothing open for negotiation, it constitutes an offer, acceptance of which will complete the contract."[49]

---

[46] 242 Va. 388, 410 S.E.2d 928 (1991).

[47] 242 Va. at 389-90, 410 S.E.2d at 929.

[48] 242 Va. at 390-91, 410 S.E.2d at 929-30.

[49] 242 Va. at 391, 410 S.E.2d at 930.

Therefore, the court held, the newspaper advertisement constituted an offer, which the Changs accepted. The fact that the ad contained a typographical error did not invalidate the contract because the bank did not inform the Changs of the mistake for three and one-half years and because "a unilateral mistake does not void an otherwise legally binding contract."[50]

Finally, it is important to note that at least one court has ruled that persons bringing actions based on allegations of false advertising may recover damages for personal injuries as well as for economic loss.[51]

---

[50] 242 Va. at 392, 410 S.E.2d at 930.

[51] Maldonado v. Nutri/System, Inc., 776 F. Supp. 278 (E.D. Va. 1991).

Chapter 10

PORNOGRAPHY

$\mathbf{F}$ew debates over free expression issues possess more passion than those related to pornography and obscenity.[1] The distribution of sexually explicit material has been the subject of two federal commissions and countless studies, experiments and lawsuits.[2]

Unfortunately, the debate over how material related to sex should be regulated or distributed in society often borders on the absurd. The works of William Shakespeare, James Joyce, John Steinbeck and William Faulkner have been attacked – along with genuine smut – as pornographic. A debate over the types of books that children could check out of the public library in one eastern North Carolina county two decades ago prompted the librarian to classify the Bible as "adult non-

---

[1] The terms "pornography" and "obscenity" are not synonymous. Pornography generally deals with material related to sex, as does erotica. While some dictionaries treat pornography and erotica as synonyms, in modern usage, erotica is generally considered to be sexual, without being degrading, while pornography is generally considered to be material that treats people – usually women – as sexual objects. Both erotica and pornography, except for child pornography, are legal in the United States. Obscene pornography, on the other hand, may be banned and distributors and producers may be punished. Pornography becomes obscene when it meets specific criteria. *See, e.g.,* discussion accompanying *infra* notes 4-5. Child pornography, that is, sexually explicit material involving persons under the age of 18, is illegal.

[2] *See, generally,* W. WAT HOPKINS, MR. JUSTICE BRENNAN AND FREEDOM OF EXPRESSION 19-49 (1991).

fiction" and require parental consent before a minor could peruse that book.

In Virginia, the absurdity has extended to Carroll County, where, in 1992, a small group of parents pushed school officials to force an English teacher to stop using an award-winning book in class, then tried to have the teacher fired. The book contained language to which the parents objected. And in 1997 prosecutors in Roanoke, because of a few vocal objections, prosecuted a nightclub operator for allowing nude dancing in a club that was closed to all persons except adults. This despite the fact that much more objectionable material was available in video stores, which remain untouched by law enforcement. The same year, a judge in Prince William County gave his stamp of approval to what was tantamount to a Star Chamber proceeding. Judge Dixon Foster allowed a prosecutor to keep secret the names of members of a committee who – by deciding whether videotapes and other materials violate community standards – helped select persons to be prosecuted on obscenity charges.[3]

These examples – few among many – demonstrate that when sexual material is involved, reason often is not.

IS IT OBSCENE?

The face of obscenity law has changed often in the United States, but since the U.S. Supreme Court's 1973 ruling in *Miller v. California*[4] the test for determining whether pornographic material is obscene has not changed. In that case, the Court held that material is obscene if it meets three criteria:

---

[3] *County 'Obscenity Pane" Members Can Remain Anonymous,* 3 NEWS MEDIA UPDATE 13 (August 25, 1997)[electronic newsletter of the Reporters Committee for Freedom of the Press, http://www.rcfp@rcfp.org].

[4] 413 U.S. 15 (1973).

(a) whether "the average person, applying contemporary community standards" would find that the work, taken as a whole, appeals to the prurient interest; . . . (b) whether the work depicts or describes in a patently offensive way, sexual conduct specifically defined by the applicable state law; and (c) whether the work, taken as a whole, lacks serious literary, artistic, political, or scientific value.[5]

A person may be punished for producing or distributing sexually explicit material only if that material is determined by a jury to be obscene, and to be obscene it must meet all three points of the Miller Test. The first point of the Miller Test invokes a local test, the second invokes a state test, and the third invokes a national test. A local jury, however, ultimately examines the material in light of all three points to determine whether it is obscene so, to some extent, all prosecutions for obscenity invoke local "contemporary community standards."

Contemporary Community Standards

In the years following the Supreme Court's first obscenity case, *Roth v. U.S.*[6] in 1957, there was some controversy among members of the Court as to whether local or national standards should apply when jurors determine whether sexually explicit material is obscene.[7] Chief Justice Warren Burger, who wrote the majority opinion in *Miller,* cleared up that controversy – though he may have initiated another. Chief

---

[5] *Id.* at 24.

[6] 354 U.S. 476 (1957).

[7] *See, e.g.,* Jacobellis v. Ohio, 478 U.S. 184, 193-95 (1964)(opinion of Brennan, J., joined by Goldberg, J.,) and 478 U.S. at 200 (Warren, C.J., dissenting).

Justice Burger made it very clear that the contemporary community standards of a local community must be considered in determining whether material is obscene. He wrote: "It is neither realistic nor constitutionally sound to read the First Amendment as requiring that the people of Maine or Mississippi accept public depiction of conduct found tolerable in Las Vegas or New York City."[8]

More than twenty-five years after *Miller,* however, courts in Virginia still have little guidance as to what "contemporary community standards" are and how they are to be applied. Two 1997 obscenity trials demonstrate the complexity and lack of understanding of the issue.

In October 1997, the owner of the nightclub Girls, Girls, Girls, Inc., was indicted on fifteen counts of violating the state's obscenity law and on fifteen counts of violating Roanoke's anti-nudity law. The attorney for Girls, Girls, Girls, Inc., attempted to introduce evidence demonstrating that the local community standards allowed for nude entertainment, but the judge in the case refused to allow the evidence. Jack Kennett wanted to show a portion of a video of the movie *Oh! Calcutta,* because a live production of the show had been performed at the Roanoke Civic Center. He also wanted to show portions of sexually explicit movies that were available for rent in local video stores. The trial judge, however, refused to admit the evidence.[9]

In addition, Assistant Commonwealth's Attorney Dennis Nagel introduced no evidence whatsoever on the question of contemporary community standards. The prosecutor simply showed jurors grainy videotapes of the nude performances at Girls, Girls, Girls, Inc.

---

[8] *Miller,* 413 U.S. at 32.

[9] Lawrence Hammack, *Yes, Nude Dancing Art, Says Scholars,* THE ROANOKE TIMES, Oct. 1, 1997, at A1.

The jury convicted the club's owner of fourteen counts of violating the anti-nudity statute, but only one count of violating the obscenity statute. Fines totaled $40,000.[10]

The clear indication is that, in Roanoke at least, jurors automatically know what contemporary community standards are.

The same is not true in Wythe County, however. Seven weeks after the Roanoke convictions, Wythe County General District Judge Daniel Bird ruled that community standards must be specified before there can be convictions for violating those standards. In the absence of evidence determining contemporary community standards, Bird ruled, six people connected with a strip show could not be convicted on obscenity related charges.[11]

Applicable State Law

The second point of the Miller Test places a unique burden upon states. It requires them to define, specifically, the types of sexual conduct that may not be depicted or described "in a patently offensive way." Without that state definition, there can be no conviction for creating or distributing obscene pornography.

By the time the Supreme Court had delivered its opinion in *Miller,* many states, including Virginia, had defined obscenity. In 1971, the Virginia General Assembly defined it this way:

> that which considered as a whole has as its dominant theme or purpose an appeal to prurient

---

[10] Lawrence Hammack, *Jury Finds No Art in 'Girls' Act; Club Fined $40,000 Maximum,* Oct. 2, 1997, at A1.

[11] Paul Dellinger, *Judge: To Convict, Wythe Must Define Standards of Obscenity,* THE ROANOKE TIMES, Nov. 25, 1997, at A1.

interest, that is, a shameful or morbid interest in nudity, sex, or excretion, and if it goes substantially beyond customary limits of candor in description or representation of such matters.[12]

The definition drew on language that appeared in *Roth v. U.S.* In *Roth,* the Court, for the first time, held that obscene material lay outside the protection of the First Amendment, and the Court defined very generally terms the term "obscenity." The Court adjusted the definition of obscenity between 1957 and 1973,[13] but in *Miller,* a majority of the Court, for the first time since *Roth,* agreed upon a new definition for the term.

Virginia's broad definition of obscenity did not change, however, and after 1973 the state statute did not appear to follow the mandate of *Miller* that definitions of obscenity be specific.

In fact, that very issue was addressed in a case called *Price v. Commonwealth.*[14] Bobby J. Price was sentenced to twelve months in prison and ordered to pay a $1,000 fine for showing the movie *Anomalies* in his Danville theater.[15] He appealed the conviction, arguing that Virginia's definition of obscenity was vague and overbroad under the *Miller* ruling.[16]

---

[12] Va. Code sec. 18.1-227 (1950).

[13] *See, e.g.,* A Book Named "John Cleland's Memoirs of a Woman of Pleasure" v. Massachusetts, 383 U.S. 413 (1966).

[14] The *Price* case demonstrates the complicated nature of the obscenity issue. The case reached the state supreme court twice before all the issues could be settled. Price v. Commonwealth, 213 Va. 113, 189 S.E.2d 324 (1972), is generally called *Price I,* and Price v. Commonwealth, 214 Va. 490, 201 S.E.2d 798 (1974) is generally called *Price II.*

[15] *Price I,* 213 Va. at 114, 189 S.E.2d at 316.

[16] *Price II,* 214 Va. at 491-92, 201 S.E.2d at 799.

The Virginia Supreme Court disagreed, holding that the statute was constitutional.[17]

The court based the ruling on its previous interpretations of the obscenity statute. Five years earlier, the court had reversed the conviction of a bookstore operator for selling copies of the magazines *Knight* and *Raw*.[18] These girlie magazines only depicted nudity, the court said, and, therefore, were not obscene.[19]

That interpretation considerably narrowed the broad nature of the obscenity statue, the Virginia Supreme Court held in *Price II*. Under the statute, therefore, only "hard core pornography" is prohibited. And, as interpreted by the court, the statue limits "hard core pornography" to "portrayals of sexual activity or excretion, not including mere nudity, which go beyond the customary limits of candor in representing such matters."[20] The statute, therefore, the court held, adheres to the requirements of *Miller* and is constitutional.

In 1975, the Virginia General Assembly altered the definition of obscenity slightly, so that it now proscribes material

> which, considered as a whole, has as its dominant theme or purpose an appeal to the prurient interest in sex, that is, a shameful or morbid interest in nudity, sexual conduct, sexual excitement, excretory functions or products thereof or sadomasochistic abuse, and which goes substantially beyond customary limits of

---

[17] *Price II,* 214 Va. at 493-94, 201 S.E.2d at 800-801.

[18] House v. Commonwealth, 210 Va. 121, 122, 169 S.E.2d 572, 573 (1969).

[19] 210 Va. at 127, 169 S.E.2d at 577.

[20] *Price II,* 214 Va. at 493, 201 S.E.2d at 800.

candor in description or representation of such matters and which, taken as a whole, does not have serious literary, artistic, political or scientific value.[21]

Serious Value

Sexually explicit material is not obscene if it contains serious value. Under *Miller,* of course, that value may be literary, artistic, political or scientific. *Miller* also requires that the work be taken as a whole when the determination of value is made. And the U.S. Supreme Court has held that the determination of value be made based on national, rather than state or local, standards.[22]

Like the first point of the Miller Test, the procedure for determining value in Virginia has a spotted history. No obscenity case turning on the issue of value has reached the Virginia Supreme Court.

Who May Sue

Virginia law prohibits obscene material in a wide variety of forms: books, pamphlets, photographs, magazines, films, videos, bumper stickers, objects or recordings.[23] It is also unlawful to exhibit any obscene object or performance,[24] to advertise any obscene performances[25] or to photograph or allow the photography of any person, including oneself, for use in

---

[21] Va. Code sec. 18.2-372 (1950).

[22] Pope v. Illinois, 418 U.S. 497 (1987).

[23] Va. Code sec. 18.2-373 (1950).

[24] Va. Code sec.18.2-375 (1950).

[25] Va. Code sec. 18.2-376 (1950).

obscene material.[26] In addition, any town, city or county can adopt additional ordinances against obscenity.[27]

The law places no restrictions on who may bring an action to determine whether material is obscene. Anyone, the law says, may petition the court to determine whether a book is obscene.[28] When such a petition is filed, a judge will examine the book to determine whether there is probable cause, and will either order a hearing to determine the obscenity of the work, or will dismiss the action. If a hearing is to be held, the judge may order that the book not be sold until after the hearing.

During the hearing, evidence may be introduced concerning the value of the book, the reaction of the public to the work, the intent and reputation of the author and publisher, the method of promoting the book and the prurient appeal of the book.

The judge must issue a written determination of his finding, which may be appealed.

REGULATING PORNOGRAPHY

Obscene material, as previously indicated, may be banned, and its producers and distributors may be punished. Material may focus on sexual matters, however, and not be

---

[26] Va. Code sec. 18.2-382 (1950).

[27] Va. Code sec. 18.2-389 (1950).

[28] Va. Code sec. 18.2-384 (1950). The Virginia statute discussed here refers only to judicial proceedings related to books. The federal appellate courts in Virginia, however, have held that films should be accorded the same protection as books, and the same type proceeding should be applied to film. *See* Tyrone v. Wilkinson, 410 F.2d 639 (4th Cir. 1969) and Greenmount Sales, Inc. v. Davila, 344 F. Supp. 860, 864 (E.D. Va. 1972), *aff'd in part and rev'd in part* 479 F.2d 591 (4th Cir. 1973).

obscene. The U.S. Supreme Court has noted that sexuality and obscenity are not synonymous.[29]

The production and distribution of pornography may be allowed by the First Amendment, but regulation of pornography is also allowed. Both the U.S. Supreme Court and the Virginia Supreme Court, for example, have held that child pornography is illegal.[30] Virginia state law prohibits both the production and possession of child pornography.[31] In addition, state law prohibits the use of communication systems such as computer networks and bulletin boards to promote child pornography.[32]

The commonwealth also prohibits the sale of sexually explicit material to minors.[33] Indeed, the commonwealth attempts to keep minors from even seeing such material on display in newsstands or bookstores. A state law requires that sexually explicit material that may be harmful to minors must be displayed in a way so that minors cannot examine that material.[34] Following a legal dispute that lasted some five years, the statute has been held to be constitutional.[35]

The commonwealth has also attempted to restrict sexually explicit material from prisoners. A federal court upheld a policy of the Keene Mountain Correctional Center in denying two prisoners copies of *Gallery* magazine.[36] The court found that sexually explicit publications have a negative impact

---

[29] *Roth,* 354 U.S. at 487.

[30] New York v. Ferber, 458 U.S. 747 (1982); Freeman v. Commonwealth, 223 Va. 301, 288 S.E.2d 461 (1982).

[31] Va. Code sec. 18.2-374.1 and sec. 18.2-374.1:1 (1950).

[32] Va. Code sec. 18.2-374.3 (1950).

[33] Va. Code sec. 18.2-391(a) (1950).

[34] *Id.*

[35] American Booksellers Association, Inc. v. Commonwealth, 882 F.2d 125 (4th Cir. 1989), *cert. denied,* 494 U.S. 1056 (1990).

[36] Hodges v. Commonwealth, 871 F. Supp. 873 (W.D. Va. 1994), *rev'd* 80 F.3d 105 (4th Cir. 1996), *cert. denied* 117 S.Ct. 296 (1996).

on the security, discipline, order, public safety and rehabilitation of prisoners.[37] The Fourth U.S. Circuit Court of appeals, however, reversed the district court's ruling, holding that the publishers of the magazines in question had a First Amendment right to present a challenge to the policy.[38]

A statute that has not been tested in court prohibits theater operators from showing previews for movies that carry motion picture ratings more restrictive than the movies being shown.[39] Under the statute, for example, a preview for an R-rated movie could not accompany the showing of a PG-13 movie.

In addition, the Virginia Supreme Court has upheld the regulation of nudity in bars and other establishments. As the experiences in Roanoke and Wythe County demonstrate, when dancers go from being topless to being completely nude, they are tempting prosecutors and are likely to face obscenity charges. It is unclear why prosecutors are singling out live performances when much more graphic sexual material is available in video stores, but the prosecutions seem to be a trend.

In addition, jurisdictions are capitalizing on a ruling by the Virginia Supreme Court allowing topless bars to be regulated. In *Wayside Restaurant, Inc. v. Virginia Beach,* the court upheld a Virginia Beach ordinance prohibiting public nudity as applied to bars.[40] The ordinance prohibited the exposing of "male or female genitals, pubic area or buttocks with less than a fully opaque covering, or the showing of the

---

[37] *Id.* at 877.

[38] Montcalm Publishing Corp. v. Beck, 80 F.3d 105 (4th Cir. 1996), *cert. denied* 519 U.S. 928 (1996).

[39] Va. Code sec. 18.2-386 (1950).

[40] 215 Va. 231, 208 S.E.2d 51 (1974).

female breast with less than a fully opaque covering of any portion thereof below the top of the nipple."[41]

In the wake of the case, a number of jurisdictions have approved ordinances prohibiting public nudity. The ordinances are aimed specifically at prohibiting topless dancing.[42]

---

[41] 215 Va. at 232, 208 S.E.2d at 52, note 1.

[42] *See, e.g.,* Kathy Loan, *Strip Club Is Back,* THE ROANOKE TIMES, January 25, 1996, at C1.

Chapter 11

STUDENT EXPRESSION IN VIRGINIA

Student expression has always held a tenuous position under the law.   As persons, students are entitled to the protections granted by the Constitution. Many students are not adults, however, so they do not enjoy full access to constitutional rights and privileges. They may not vote, for example, buy alcoholic beverages or drive cars until they reach legally specified ages.

Similarly, in many circumstances, they are not allowed to express themselves with the full vigor that adults enjoy. The U.S. Supreme Court has recognized that young people enjoy the right of free expression and, to paraphrase the Court, that they do not shed that right at the schoolhouse gate.[1]   But other factors govern the degree and extent of student speech. While young people are at school, for example, the elementary and high school administrators and teachers under whose care those young people fall, operate *in loco parentis* – in the place of parents. The law recognizes that these school officials can exercise some control over students – including the way students express themselves – in order to ensure that the function of the school setting is maintained and the students are insulated from inappropriate material.

----

[1] Tinker v. Des Moines School District, 393 U.S. 503, 506 (1969).

While recognizing the free speech rights of students, therefore, the Court has also allowed school officials to restrict and punish offensive speech.[2] The Court has also held that a principal has the authority to unilaterally censor a high school newspaper if the principal does not believe material in the newspaper fits into the pedagogical goals of the school.[3] But, while expressive conduct on school grounds may be restricted,[4] courts have been reluctant to prohibit the distribution of literature unless there is a likelihood the distribution will cause disruption.[5]

In general, speech issues involving students fall into two categories: freedom of the student press and free speech rights on school property.

FREEDOM OF THE HIGH SCHOOL PRESS

In the 1988 case *Hazelwood School District v. Kuhlmeier,* the U.S. Supreme Court ruled that a principal could censor a high school newspaper because he believed the material published in the newspaper to be inappropriate for students in his school. The principal pulled two pages from the school paper without consulting either student editors or the newspaper's advisor.[6]

---

[2] *See, e.g.,* Bethel School Dist. v. Fraser, 478 U.S. 675 (1986).

[3] Hazelwood School Dist. v. Kuhlmeier, 484 U.S. 260 (1988).

[4] Crosby v. Holsinger, 852 F.2d 801 (4th Cir. 1988).

[5] Baughman v. Freienmuth, 478 F.2d 1345 (4th Cir. 1973); Quarterman v. Byrd, 453 F.2d 54 (4th Cir. 1971). *Baughman* is a Maryland case, and *Quarterman* is a North Carolina case, but both opinions are from the Fourth Circuit, which also holds jurisdiction over Virginia. *See also* Leibner v. Sharbaugh, 429 F. Supp. 744 (E.D. Va. 1977).

[6] 484 U.S. at 261.

Until that ruling, the high school press enjoyed significant freedom. Many courts, including the Fourth U.S. Circuit Court of Appeals, which holds jurisdiction over Virginia, ruled that high school newspapers were public forums and could not be regulated by school administrators on the basis of content.[7]

Much has changed, however.

Since *Hazelwood,* the Student Press Law Center of Washington, D.C., which is dedicated to freedom of the student press, has reported an increase in the number of calls from student editors facing administrative censorship.[8] In addition, anecdotal evidence from across Virginia indicates that school administrators are taking a more aggressive role in controlling the student press.[9]

The Student Press Law Center recommends that high school editors combat potential censorship in two ways. First, the Center recommends that editors encourage state legislators to pass legislation protecting the high school press from unwarranted censorship. The Center has developed model legislation that can be sent to legislators which, if passed, would protect school-sponsored publications, even if those publications are published in conjunction with classes.

The legislation allows regulation of obscenity, defamation, invasion of privacy and material that would cause a substantial disruption at school, but gives student editors protection in determining the news, opinion and advertising

---

[7] Gambino v. Fairfax County School Board, 564 F.2d 157 (4th Cir. 1977), *affirming* 429 F. Supp. 731 (E.D. Va. 1977).

[8] The address of the Student Press Law Center is Suite 504, 1735 Eye Street, NW, Washington, D.C. 20006; the phone number is (202) 466-5242.

[9] *See, e.g., Advisor submits to prior review policy,* SPLC REPORT 25 (Winter 1989-90).

content of their publications and prohibits prior review of student publications by administrators.

The Student Press Law Center also recommends that student publications specifically identify themselves as public forums for student expression. The Center reports that the Supreme Court indicated that "if the Hazelwood School District had been operating under a policy that described its student publications as forums for student expression, it would not have allowed non-disruptive stories about teen pregnancy and divorce to be censored."[10]

Copies of the model legislation and model guidelines for identification as a public forum are available from the Student Press Law Center and are published in *Law of the Student Press,* a handbook published by the Center.[11]

FREEDOM OF THE UNIVERSITY PRESS

The Supreme Court's ruling in *Hazelwood* does not affect the student press at public universities, at least not in Virginia and other states within the Fourth U.S. Circuit Court of Appeals. That court ruled in a North Carolina case that the student press at public universities operates as a public forum and may not be regulated by university officials, even if mandatory student fees pay for the production of the newspaper.[12]

While *Hazelwood* overruled similar rulings as they applied to the high school press, rulings related to universities remain intact. Student newspapers that are not part of a

---

[10] STUDENT PRESS LAW CENTER, LAW OF THE STUDENT PRESS 96 (1985).

[11] The Student Press Law Center model legislation is found in LAW OF THE STUDENT PRESS at 94; guidelines for designing a student newspaper as a public forum are found at 97. *See supra* note 8.

[12] Joyner v. Whiting, 477 F.2d 456 (4th Cir. 1973).

university's curriculum, therefore, may not be censored and may not be subjected to prior review by administrators.

In addition, the Supreme Court, in 1994, affirmed the proposition that student publications at public universities could not be denied funding on the basis of content – even if the content is religious. *Rosenberger v. Rector and Visitors of the University of Virginia*[13] is an important case for advocates of free speech for students.

The case began when Wide Awake Productions, a student organization at the University of Virginia, sought funding for its publication, *Wide Awake: A Christian Perspective at the University of Virginia.* The funding was denied on grounds that the publication promoted a Christian viewpoint. Attorneys for the university argued that the university had limited funding and was required to establish some mechanism for distributing those limited funds. One method, the university argued, was denying funds to organizations that used publications to promote religious viewpoints.[14] The U.S. Supreme Court, however, ruled that the university could not use viewpoint discrimination as a basis for distributing funds.[15] To do so, the Court held, violates the First Amendment.[16]

Newspapers at private colleges and universities, however, enjoy significantly less freedom. Private colleges and universities are not considered to be part of the government; they operate on private rather than public funds. The First Amendment of the Constitution restricts the state from abridging the freedom of the press, but not private institutions,

---

[13] 515 U.S. 819 (1994).

[14] *Id.* at 832-33.

[15] *Id.* at 835.

[16] *Id.* at 837.

so private colleges and universities can presume to be publishers of student newspapers. Administrators, therefore, have authority to replace editors, fire advisors and control the content of the student press. While this may be pedagogically unsound, it is legal.[17]

Student editors at public institutions might have significant freedom from regulations imposed by their colleges or universities, but because of their independence they are increasingly the targets of lawsuits. Indeed, the *Collegiate Times*, the student newspaper at Virginia Tech, faced two lawsuits in 1997, both of which were resolved in 1998.

Sharon Yeagle, a mid-level administrator at Tech, sued the newspaper when editors forgot to change a line in a template used to design the newspaper and, as a result, she was identified as "Director of Butt Licking."[18] The line appeared under Yeagle's name in a graphic display of a quotation accompanying a news story. When the template was used to set off the quote, editors failed to replace the line with Yeagle's actual title, assistant to the vice president of student affairs. Editors attempted to apologize to Yeagle, who refused to talk to them and, instead, sued for defamation. The Virginia Supreme Court upheld a circuit court ruling dismissing the case because, in the words of the supreme court, "the phrase at issue could not reasonably be considered as conveying factual information."[19]

The second suit against the *Collegiate Times* was filed by Tony Morrison, a former football player at Tech who was charged with but never indicted for rape. Morrison sued the paper for an editorial critical of the administration's handling of

---

[17] For a discussion of the pedagogical ramifications of student press restrictions, *see* W. Wat Hopkins, *Hazelwood v. Kuhlmeier: Sound Constitutional Law, Unsound Pedagogy,* 16 N. KY. L. REV. 521 (1989).

[18] Yeagle v. Collegiate Times, 255 Va. 293, 497 S.E.2d 136, 137 (1998).

[19] 255 Va. at 298, 497 S.E. at 139.

the case. He claimed that the editorial falsely charged him with committing a crime.[20]   In May 1998, the suit was dismissed on a motion by Morrison's attorney.[21]

While both suits border on the ludicrous, they demonstrate that student journalists are not immune from legal action simply because they are students.

FREEDOM OF STUDENT EXPRESSION

The courts allow school administrators significant leeway in controlling access to school property for the purpose of expressive conduct and control of what may be called school-sponsored speech.

Federal courts in Virginia, for example, have ruled that school officials had the right to ban the "Johnny Reb" symbol as a school mascot because the symbol was offensive to blacks at the school[22] and suspend a student for wearing a shirt saying "Drugs Suck!"[23]

Virginia courts have also ruled that high school principals may ban from campus students who participated in disruptive conduct – such as sit-ins or protests.   And those students who do not leave campuses when ordered to do so may be charged with trespassing.[24] The same is true for colleges and

---

[20] Morrison v. Padalino, 760 CL 96 B02902-00 (Richmond Circuit, Filed Nov. 27, 1996).

[21] Ian Zack, *Ex-Player's Newspaper Suit Dismissed,* THE ROANOKE TIMES, May 6, 1998, at B4.

[22] Crosby v. Holsinger, 852 F.2d 801 (4th Cir. 1989).

[23] Broussard v. School Board of Norfolk, 801 F. Supp. 1526 (E.D. Va. 1992).

[24] Pleasants v. Commonwealth, 214 Va. 646, 203 S.E.2d 114 (1974).

universities.[25]   University restrictions on expressive conduct, however, must be content neutral[26] and must allow demonstrations at some locations on campus.[27]

Colleges and universities also have authority to control access to campuses, even when the purpose of access is simply to express opinions. Virginia Tech refused to grant an itinerant preacher permission to preach on the university's Drill Field because the preacher, James G. Gilles, was not sponsored by an individual or group affiliated with the university. Circumventing university policy, officials gave Gilles permission to preach at the school's outdoor amphitheater, a secluded spot that received little traffic. Gilles sued, but the Fourth U.S. Circuit Court of Appeals refused to rule on the merits of the case. The court held that Gilles could not show that he had been prevented from preaching because he could not gain sponsorship.[28]

The court recognized that it was dancing around the issue, but blamed the parties for prompting an opinion that was technical rather than substantive:

> We do not foreclose the possibility that some justiciable
> case will arise between these parties in the future. At that
> time, however, the record may reveal what it does not
> reveal now – namely, the reasons for denying Gilles access
> to the precise forum he sought and his precise challenge to
> those reasons. As it is, the parties are jousting over a
> sponsorship requirement that is not being invoked to bar

---

[25] Johnson v. Commonweath, 212 Va. 579, 186 S.E.2d 53 (1972), *cert. denied,* 407 U.S. 925 (1972).

[26] Students Against Apartheid Coalition v. O'Neil, 838 F.2d 735 (4th Cir. 1988).

[27] Sword v. Fox, 446 F.2d 1091 (4th Cir. 1971), *cert. denied,* 404 U.S. 994 (1971).

[28] Gilles v. Torgersen, 71 F.3d 497, 499 (4th Cir. 1995).

Gilles from speaking on campus, and they are ignoring whatever time, place or manner guideline is presumably being used to prohibit him from speaking on the drillfield. In other words, the true controversy is eluding the court, while a false one is proposed.[29]

Despite the court's disclaimer, Gilles was denied the right to preach on the Drill Field simply because officials at a major university said he couldn't do so.

Had Gilles chosen to distribute handbills on or around the Drill Field announcing that he would later be preaching at the amphitheater, however, he would likely have been able to do so. Not even high school principals have the right to ban the distribution of literature at their schools, unless regulations are narrowly drawn and specific as to the types of literature that may not be distributed.[30]

In addition, as demonstrated in *Rosenberger*, courts have been hesitant to limit student expression on the basis of content, even when the expression is obnoxious. When the Sigma Chi Fraternity at George Mason University held an womanless beauty contest, for example, in which members of the fraternity portrayed stereotypical images of different types of women, the university responded by suspending the fraternity and placing it on a two-year probation.[31] The Fourth U.S. Circuit Court of Appeals called the performance "an exercise of teenage campus excess,"[32] but held, nevertheless,

---

[29] *Id.* at 501.

[30] *See* cases cited at *supra* note 5.

[31] Iota Xi Chapter of Sigma Chi Fraternity v. George Mason University, 933 F.2d 386, 388 (4th Cir. 1993).

[32] *Id.* at 389.

that it was still inherently expressive and, thus, entitled to First Amendment protection.[33]

---

[33] *Id.* at 390.

FOR ADDITIONAL READING

Articles

Anderson, David. "The Origins of the Press Clause." 20 *UCLA Law Review* 455 (1983).

Hopkins, W. Wat. "Hazelwood v. Kulhmeier:Sound Constitutional Law, Unsound Pedagogy." 16 *Northern Kentucky Law Review* 521 (1989).

——"Negligence Ten Years After Gertz v. Welch." *Journalism Monographs*, No. 93 (August 1985).

Kohler, David C. "Toward a Modern Defamation Law in Virginia:Questions Answered, Questions Raised." 21 *University of Richmond Law Review* 3 (Fall 1986).

Okuda, Sue S. "Criminal Antiprofit Laws:Some Thoughts in Favor of Their Constitutionality." 76 *California Law Review* 1353 (1988).

Roach, Phillip Randolph Jr. "The Newsman's Confidential Source Privilege in Virginia." 22 *University of Richmond Law Review* 377 (1988).

Warren, Samuel and Louis Brandeis. "The Right of Privacy." 4 *Harvard Law Review* 193 (1890).

Books & Book Chapters

Franklin, Marc A. *The Biography of a Legal Dispute*. Mineola, N.Y.:Foundation Press, 1984.

Hermanson, Louise. "The Law in Modern Society" in *Communication and the Law*, W. Wat Hopkins, ed. Northport, Ala.: Vision Press, 1998.

Hopkins, W. Wat. *Actual Malice Twenty-Five Years After Times v. Sullivan*. New York:Praeger, 1989.

—   *Mr. Justice Brennan and Freedom of Expression*. New York:Praeger, 1991.

Howard, A.E. Dick. *Commentaries on the Constitution of Virginia*. Charlottesville:University Press of Virginia, 1974.

Law of the Student Press. Washington, D.C.:Student Press Law Center, 1985.

Levy, Leonard. *Emergence of a Free Press*. New York:Oxford University Press, 1985.

Middleton, Kent R., Bill F. Chamberlin and Matthew D. Bunker. *The Law of Public Communication*. New York:Longwood, 1997.

Moore, Roy L. *Mass Communication Law and Ethics*. Hillsdale, N.J.:Lawrence Erlbaum, 1994.

Myers, Marvin, ed. *The Mind of the Founder*. Hanover, N.H.: Brandeis University Press, 1981.

Overbeck, Wayne. *Major Principles of Media Law*. New York: Holt, Rinehart and Winston, 1996.

Pember, Don R. *Mass Media Law*. Dubuque, Iowa:W.C. Brown, 1997.

Schwartz, Bernard. *The Bill of Rights: A Documentary History*. New York:Chelsea House, 1971.

Walden, Ruth. "Access to Courts," in *Communication and the Law*, W. Wat Hopkins, ed. Northport, Ala.:Vision Press, 1998.

Wellford, Alexander and David C. Kohler. "Survey of Virginia Defamation Law" *in LDRC 50-State Survey*. New York:Libel Defense Resource Center, 1992.

Youm, Kyu Ho. "The Plaintiff's Case," in *Communication and the Law*, W. Wat Hopkins, ed. Northport, Ala.:Vision Press, 1998.

Miscellaneous

"Confidential Sources and Information, A Practical Guide for Reporters in the 50 States, Pull-out Section." *The News Media and the Law*, Fall 1990.

General Information Relating to the Courts Within Each Circuit and District in Virginia. Richmond:Office of the Executive Secretary, Supreme Court of Virginia, 1997.

Keller, Teresa. *Cameras in Courtrooms: An Analysis of Television Court Coverage in Virginia.* Unpublished doctoral dissertation, University of Tennessee, Knoxville, 1992.

News Media Handbook on Virginia Law and Courts. Richmond: Virginia Bar Association, 1992.

Reporter's Handbook on Media Law. Richmond:Virginia Press Association, 1990 ed.

Restatement (Second) of Torts. St. Paul:American Law Institute, 1977.

Riley, Sam. *The Free Press-Fair Trial Controversy: A Discussion of the Issues Involved and an Examination of Pre-Trial Publicity by Survey Research.* Unpublished doctoral dissertation, University of North Carolina at Chapel Hill, 1970.

Virginia Courts in Brief. Richmond:Office of the Executive Secretary, Supreme Court of Virginia.

Virginia Coalition for Open Government web page. http//www.gateway-va.com/opengovt/index.htm.

Virginia Court System web page. http//www.courts.state.va.us/.

Mass Communication Law in Virginia

CASE INDEX

Charlottesville Newspapers, Inc. v. Matthews, 53 n. 18, 59, 60 nn. 45-46, 78

Chaves v. Johnson, 89 n. 171, 90 nn. 173 & 175, 91 n. 176, 92 n. 186

Chesapeake and Ohio Railway Company v. Hanes, 61 n. 51

Chuy v. Philadelphia Eagles Football Club, 113 n. 39

Cobb v. Rector and Visitors of the University of Virginia, 51 n. 11

Cohen v. Cowles Media, Inc., 143

Coppola v. Commonwealth, 152 n. 32

Costlow v. Cusimano, 113 n. 44

Crawford v. United Steel Workers, AFL-CIO, 58 n. 38

Crosby v. Holsinger, 184 n. 4, 187 n. 22

D

Davis v. Heflin, 49 n. 4, 51 n. 11

Dean v. Town of Elkton, 56 nn. 29-31

Dotti v. Virginia Board of Medicine, 166 n. 41

Dwyer v. Smith, 49 n. 5, 51 n. 12

E

Edwards v. National Audubon Society, Inc., 98 n. 205

Edwards v. New York Times Co., 98 n. 205

Ewell v. Boutwell, 55 n. 27, 62 n. 63

F

Falwell v. Flynt, 104 n. 13, 114 nn. 47-48

Falwell v. Penthouse International, Ltd., 100 n. 4, 103 n. 12, 104 n. 13

Federated Publications v. Swedberg, 153 n. 36

Ferguson v. Commonwealth, 41 nn. 70-71

Fitzgerald v. Penthouse International, Ltd., 69 n. 97, 82 n. 145

Fleming v. Moore, 49 n. 3, 50 n. 9, 53 n. 18, 58 n. 40, 68 n. 93, 72 nn. 108-09, 82

Food Lion, Inc. v. Melton, 51 n. 12, 61 n. 57

Foretich v. Capital Cities/ABC, Inc., 72 n. 110

Freedlander v. Edens Broadcasting, Inc., 54, 56, 60, 60 nn. 48-49, 61 n. 50, 69 n. 94, 70 nn. 99 & 100

Freeman v. Commonwealth, 178 n. 30

G

Galella v. Onassis, 113 n. 40

Gambino v. Fairfax County School Board, 183 n. 7

Gazette, Inc. v. Harris, 50 n. 9, 53, 58 nn. 40-41, 59, 60 nn. 45-46, 63 n. 67, 65 n. 77, 75 nn. 121 & 125, 76 n. 126, 76, 77-78, 79 nn. 134-36, 82, 82 nn. 147-48, 84 n. 149, 87 n. 164, 95 n. 197

General Products Co. v. Meredith Corp., 72 n. 107

Gertz v. Robert Welch, Inc., 66 n. 83, 69 nn. 94 & 96, 72, 72 n. 111, 97 n. 200

Gilbert v. Allied Chemical Corporation, 139 n. 15, 141 n. 25

Gilles v. Torgersen, 188 n. 28, 189 n. 29

Gray v. Commonwealth, 152 n. 32

Great Coastal Express, Inc. v. Ellington, 59 nn. 42-44, 65 nn. 78 & 80, 88 n. 163

Greenmount Sales, Inc. v. Davila, 177 n. 28

Griffin v. Shively, 74 n. 119

H

Hale v. Washington County School Board, 127

Hall v. Commonwealth, 40 n. 64, 109 n. 29

Hazelwood School District v. Kuhlmeier, 176-84, 182 n. 3

Henry v. R.C. Chevrolet, Inc., 160 n. 4
Hernandez v. Superintendent,
    Fredericksburg-Rappahonnock Joint
    Security Center, 44 n. 83
Hershfield v. Commonwealth, 45 n. 87
Hertz v. Times-World Corp., 151 nn 26-
    28
Hines v. Gravins, 49 n. 4
Hodges v. Commonwealth, 36 n. 42, 178
    n. 36, 179 n. 37
Hood v. Naeter Brothers Publishing Co.,
    113 n. 42
House v. Commonwealth, 175 n. 18-19
Hustler Magazine v. Falwell, 112 n. 36,
    114, 115 nn. 49-50

I

In re Times-World Corp., 148 n. 12, 150
    n. 22-24
In re Worrell Enterprises, Inc., 150 n. 22,
    151 n. 25
Iota Xi Chapter of Sigma Chi Fraternity
    v. George Mason University, 189 nn.
    31-33

J

Jacobellis v. Ohio, 171 n. 7
James v. Haymes, 63 n. 69, 85 n. 154, 91
    n. 182, 93 n. 187
Johnson v. Commonwealth, 108 n. 26,
    188 n. 25
Joyner v. Whiting, 184 n. 12

K

Kilgore v. Younger, 113 n. 43
Kroger Company v. Young, 87 n. 162

L

Landmark Communications v. Common-
    wealth, 26 n. 2, 30
Landmark Communications, Inc. v.
    Macione, 65 n. 76

Landmark Communications v. Virginia,
    9 n. 24, 30 n. 18, 31
Lapkoff v. Wilks, 91 n. 179, 91 n. 183
LaRouche v. National Broadcasting Co.,
    139, 141
Lavery v. Automation Management
    Consultants, Inc., 101 n. 9, 102 n. 10
Lee v. The Dong-A-Ilbo, 88 n. 167
Lee Art Theatre, Inc. v. Virginia, 9 n. 27
Leibner v. Sharbaugh, 182 n. 5
Leonard v. Fields, 31
Letter Carriers, AFL-CIO v. Austin, 9 n.
    28, 95 nn. 193-94

M

M. Rosenberg & Sons v. Croft, 57 n. 35,
    58 n. 36
Mainstream Loudoun v. Board of
    Trustees of the Loudoun County
    Library, 38 nn. 52-54
Maldonado v. Nutri/Systems, Inc., 167 n.
    51
Maressa v. New Jersey Monthly, 136 n. 3
Marsh v. Richmond Newspapers, Inc.,
    131 n. 32, 133 n. 39
McBride v. Roanoke Redevelopment and
    Housing Authority, 31, 62 n. 62, 96
    n. 198
McIntyre v. Ohio Elections Commission,
    164 n. 35
Mercer v. Winston, 45 n. 86
Miami Herald v. Tornillo, 81 n. 144
Milkovich v. Lorain Journal, 89
Miller v. California, 170-76
Miller v. National Broadcasting Co., 113
    n. 41
Mills v. Kingsport Times-News, 58 n. 36
Montcalm Publishing Corp. v. Beck, 36
    nn. 42-43, 179 n. 38
Montgomery Ward v. Nance, 61 n. 56,
    87 n. 162
Morrisey v. William Morrow & Co., Inc.,
    84 nn. 152-53

Morrison v. Collegiate Times, 66 n. 82
Morrison v. Padalino, 187 n. 20
Motsinger v. Kelly, 91 n. 180

N

NAACP v. Button, 9 n. 29
National Foundation for Center
    Research, Inc. v. Council for Better
    Business Bureaus, Inc., 70, 70 nn.
    101-02, 91 n. 178, 93 n. 188
Near v. Minnesota, 25 n. 1
Nebraska Press Association v. Stuart, 81
    n. 144, 153 n. 37
New York v. Ferber, 178 n. 30
New York Times Co. v. Sullivan, 2 n. 3,
    9 n. 22, 56, 74 n. 116, 95, 115 n. 49
Newspaper Publishing Corp. v. Burke,
    81-82

O

Old Dominion Branch 496 v. Austin, 92
    n. 185, 94 n. 190, 95 nn. 191-92
O'Mara v. Commonwealth, 43, 43 n. 80
O'Neil v. Edmonds, 58 n. 37
Owens v. Commonwealth, 41 nn. 70-71

P

Parker v. Commonwealth, 45 n. 90
Parr v. Commonwealth, 61 n. 54
Pell v. Procunier, 135 n. 2
Penick v. Ratcliffe, 86 nn. 156-57
Perkins v. Commonwealth, 45 n. 89, 116
    n. 55
Perlin v. Chappell, 74 n. 119
Philadelphia Newspapers v. Hepps, 95-
    96
Philip Morris Companies v. American
    Broadcasting Companies, 140 nn. 18
    & 20
Pike v. Eubank, 61 n. 54
Pilkenton v. Kingsport Publishing Co.,
    64 n. 71
Pleasants v. Commonwealth, 187 n. 24

Pope v. Commonwealth, 152 n. 32
Pope v. Illinois, 176 n. 22
Port Packet Corp. v. Lewis, 53, 56, 79
    nn. 134-36
Potomac Valve & Fitting, Inc. v.
    Crawford Fitting Co., 90 n. 174
Powell v. Young, 61 n. 55
Press-Enterprise Co. v. Superior Court,
    150 n. 22
Price v. Commonwealth, 174, 174 nn.
    14-16, 175, 175 nn. 17 & 20
Pruitt v. Wilder, 33
PSINET v. Chapman, 38 nn. 55-56

Q

Quarterman v. Byrd, 182 n. 5

R

R.A.V. v. St. Paul, Minnesota, 42 n. 77,
    43 n. 78
Renwick v. News & Observer Publishing
    Co., 100 n. 3
Reuber v. Food Chemical News, Inc., 71
    nn. 103-04, 98 nn. 203-05
Richmond Newspapers, Inc. v. Com-
    monwealth (Richmond Newspapers
    II), 147-48
Richmond Newspapers, Inc. v.
    Lipscomb, 65 n. 77, 67-68, 75, 79-83
Richmond Newspapers, Inc. v. Virginia
    (Richmond Newspapers I), 9 n. 25,
    147-49
Rideau v. Louisiana, 152 n. 30
Rinehart v. Toledo Blace Co., 100 n. 3
Roanoke School Board v. Times-World
    Corp., 132 n. 34
Robert v. Norfolk, 26 n. 3, 39 nn. 59-60
Rosenberger v. Rector and Trustees,
    University of Virginia, 32, 185, 189
Ross v. Burns, 113 n. 45
Roth v. U.S., 25 n. 1, 171, 174, 178 n.
    29
Rushford v. The New Yorker Magazine,
    88 nn. 164-65

S

Saleeby v. Free Press, Inc., 63 n. 69, 96 n. 199

Sanders v. Harris (Times-World Corporation), 87 n. 159

Seabolt v. Westmoreland Coal Co., 96 n. 198

Shah v. Medical Economics Co., 56 n. 28

Shenandoah Publishing House, Inc. v. Fanning, 151 n. 29

Shenandoah Publishing House, Inc. v. Gunter, 63 n. 68

Shenandoah Publishing House, Inc. v. Shenandoah County Board of Supervisors, 129 n. 28

Shupe v. Roses' Stores, 49 n. 3, 49 n. 6, 57 n. 33, 62 n. 61

Simon & Schuster, Inc. v. New York Crime Victims Board, 33 n. 36

Skull v. Virginia, 9 n. 26

Smalls v. Wright, 87 n. 161

Southwestern Tidewater Opportunity Project, Inc. v. Bade, 88 n. 163

State v. Sandstrom, 136 n. 3

Stickels v. General Rental Co., 139 n. 15, 141 n. 26, 143 n. 27

Stockton v. Commonwealth, 152 n. 32, 153 n. 34

Story v. Norfolk-Portsmouth Newspapers, Inc., 51 n. 13, 85 n. 155

Students Against Apartheid Coalition v. O'Neil, 188 n. 26

Swengler v. ITT Corporation Electro-Optical Products Division, 61 n. 58

Sword v. Fox, 188 n. 27

T

Tasker v. Commonwealth, 59 n. 43

Taylor v. Worrell Enterprises, Inc., 121 n. 13, 126 n. 21

Texas v. Johnson, 41 n. 72

Thomas v. Danville, 41 nn. 68-69

Times-Dispatch Publishing Co., Inc. v. Zoll, 87 n. 158, 88 n. 166

Tinker v. Des Moines School District, 181 n. 1

Town & Country Properties, Inc. v. Riggins, 100 n. 4, 105 nn. 16-18

Tull v. Brown, 121 n. 14, 123 nn. 16-17

Tyrone v. Wilkinson, 177 n. 28

U

United States v. Eichmann, 42 n. 75

United States v. Model Magazine Distributors, Inc., 137 n. 8

Urofsky v. Allen, 36 n. 44, 37 nn. 46-50

V

Vesco v. New Way Enterprises, Ltd., 112 n. 38

Virginia State Pharmacy Board v. Virginia Citizens Consumer Council, 29, 30 n. 16

W

Wall v. Fairfax County School Board, 125, 125 n. 19

Wayside Restaurant, Inc. v. Virginia Beach, 179-80

Weaver v. Beneficial Finance Co., 52 n. 14

Wells v. Liddy, 73 nn. 112-15

Weston v. Commonwealth, 146 n. 4

Wilder v. Johnson Publishing Co., 57 n. 34

Williams v. Garraghty, 92 n. 184

Williams Printing Company v. Saunders, 86 n. 156

Winegard v. Oxberger, 136 n. 3

Womack v. Eldridge, 112 n. 35

Y

Yeagle v. Collegiate Times, 64 n. 72, 64
    nn. 73-75, 1186 nn. 18-19
York v. Danville, 40 nn. 62-63

Z

Zayre of Virginia, Inc. v. Gowdy, 61 n.
    57, 62 n. 64

SUBJECT INDEX

Fourth U.S. Circuit Court of Appeals, 20, 24, 32, 36, 37, 40, 52, 69, 70, 71, 72, 84, 98, 139, 165, 179, 183, 184, 188, 187
Frederick Cancer Research Institute, 70
free circulation newspapers, 166
Free Lance Star, 139
free-lance journalists, 102
Freedlander, Eric M., 54
Freedom of Information Act,
    see Virginia Freedom of Information Act
Freedom to Access to Clinic Entrances Act, 40

G

gag orders, 155
Gallery magazine, 179
Gay and Straight Citizens of Southwest Virginia, 27
Gazette (Goochland County), 76-77
George Mason University, 189
Gilles, James G., 189-90
Gilmore, James S., 164
Girls, Girls, Girls, Inc., 172
Goochland County, 76
Government Data Collection and Dissemination Practices Act, 101
government employees and speech, 31-32, 36-38
grand juries, 118
Grubb, Ray, 64
"Guidelines for Release of Information to the News Media," 153

H

Hallock, David, 119
handbills, 40-41
Harris, James, 76-77
Harris, Virginia, 76-77
Heritage Preservation Association, 27
high school press, 182-86
Hopkins, W. Wat, 119

Houck, R. Edward, 119
House of Delegates, Virginia,
    see Virginia House of Delegates
House of Representatives, U.S., 5, 6
Hughes, Melvin R., 104
Human Rights Act, 124
Hustler magazine, 114

I

indecent language, 45
    see also fighting words, insulting words, threatening language
insulting words, 47-49, 100, 115-16
    see also fighting words, indecent language, threatening language
intentional infliction of emotional distress, 100, 110-15
Internet, 38
intrusion, 100, 105-10
invasion of privacy, 99-101
    see also appropriation, intentional infliction of emotional distress, intrusion, insulting words, Privacy Protection Act, peeping Tom statutes, photography and invasion of privacy, private information, private property, trespassing, false light invasion of privacy

J

James Madison University, 73
Jefferson, Thomas, 90
Johnson, Randall, 132-33
Joyce, James, 169
Judicial Inquiry and Review Commission, 30, 32
juries, *see* grand juries, petit juries

K

Keeler, Donna Leigh, 54
Keene Mountain Correctional Center, 179
Kennett, Jack, 172
Kinser, Cynthia D., 151

picketing, 40, 106
pornography
    child, 178
    computer, 36-38, 178
    hard core, 175
    regulations, 177-80
    see also, dancing, nude; obscenity;
        topless bars
Powell, Lewis, 137
President, U.S., 8
Price, Bobby, J., 174
Prince William County, 170
prisoners, 36
privacy, invasion of,
    see invasion of privacy
Privacy Protection Act, 100
    see also invasion of privacy
private information, publication of, 100,
    113
    see also, invasion of privacy
private people, 66
private property and newsgathering, 109
    and signs, 165
    see also picketing
privilege, 83
    absolute, 85
    and broadcasters, 88
    and falsity, 87-88
    and opinion, 92-95
    and public records, 86-87
    qualified, 85-88
Prosser, William, 99
Pruitt, Dan F., 33
public demonstrations, *see* picketing
public figures, 68-74, 112, 114
public forums, 183, 184
public meetings, 128-32
    see also closed meetings, Virginia
        Freedom of Information Act
public officials, 67-68, 112
public records, *see* law enforcement
    records; privilege and public records;
    records, official; Virginia Freedom of
    Information Act

Q

qualified privilege,
    see privilege, qualified

R

Raw magazine, 175
records, official, 120-27
    see also law enforcement records,
        Virginia Freedom of Information Act
Republicans, 8
Resolutions for Proposing Independence,
    2
Restatement (Second) of Torts, 99, 112
Reuber, Melvin, 70-71
Revolutionary War,
    see American Revolution
Richmond, 20, 54, 104, 140
Richmond Times-Dispatch, 66, 78
Riggins, John, 104-05
Riggins, Mary Lou, 104
riots,
    see unlawful assemblies
Roanoke, 20, 114, 170, 172-73
Roanoke City School Board, 132
Roanoke Civic Center, 172
Roanoke Times (& World-News), 52

S

Schwartz, Bernard, 3
Science Museum of Virginia, 129, 130
Sedition Act of 1798, 2, 8
Senate, U.S., 6
Shakespeare, William, 169
shield laws, 136-377
Sigma Chi fraternity, 189
Sixth Amendment, U.S. Constitution,
    145, 148
slander, 48-49
soliciting,
    see door-to-door solicitations,
        telephone solicitations
"Son-of-Sam" statutes, 33-35
sources, confidential,
    see confidentiality

South Carolina, 20
Speaker of the House, 6
Sports Illustrated, 102-03
St. Paul, Minn., 42
stalking, 45
Star Chamber, 170
Steinbeck, John, 169
Stewart, Potter, 138-40, 141
strict scrutiny, 38
Student Press Law Center, 183-84
students, free speech for, 175-76
 see also, college press, high school
  press
Supreme Court of the United States, 23-
  24, 25, 28, 30, 31-32, 33, 34-35, 41,
  42, 66, 72, 81, 83, 89, 93, 95, 98,
  114, 135, 138, 139, 143, 147,
  148, 149, 152, 153, 159, 164, 170,
  171,173-74, 176, 178, 181-82, 185
Supreme Court of Virginia, 18, 19, 23,
  25, 26, 29, 30, 40, 43, 52, 53, 58, 59,
  60, 62, 63, 64, 65, 67, 75, 77, 81, 82,
  83, 85, 89, 90, 91, 92, 96, 101, 104-
  05, 108, 110, 118,122-23,125, 127,
  131,138, 143, 146,
  147-48, 151,152, 155, 166-68, 175,
  176, 179, 180, 186
Surry County Circuit Court, 123
swastika, 43-44
Sweeny, Barbara H., 76-77

T

telephone pay-per-service operations,
 163
telephone solicitations, 106, 163
Texas, 41-42
Thomas Jefferson Center for the
 Protection of Free Expression, 27
Thomas Jefferson High School (Richmond), 67
threatening language, 45
 see also fighting words, indecent
  language, insulting words, 47-48
time, place and manner restrictions,

topless bars, 179-80
 see also dancing, nude
Toxic Substances Information Act, 124
trespassing, 100, 107-08
trials,
 see courts

U

U.S. Circuit Courts,
 see Fourth U.S. Circuit Court of
  Appeals
U.S. District Court for the Eastern
  District of Virginia, 20, 30, 33, 37,
  38, 52, 54, 69
U.S. District Court for the Western
  District of Virginia, 20, 31, 32, 36,
  38, 103
U.S. Supreme Court,
 see Supreme Court of the United
  States
Uhrig, Roland, 79
United Press International, 157
University of Virginia, 32, 58, 81, 125,
  185
unlawful assemblies, 41

V

venue, change of, 152
Vice President, U.S., 6
Virginia, University of,
 see University of Virginia,
Virginia Association of Broadcasters,
  156-57
Virginia Attorney General, 128, 132
Virginia Beach, 179
Virginia Board of Corrections, 130
Virginia Board of Elections, 164
Virginia Coalition for Open Government,
  120
Virginia Code,
 see Code of Virginia
Virginia common law,
 see common law, common law
  malice

About the Author

W. Wat Hopkins, Ph.D., is an associate professor of communication studies at Virginia Tech, where he teaches journalism and communication law courses. He has a master's degree in journalism and a Ph.D. degree in mass communication research, both from the University of North Carolina at Chapel Hill. He was a reporter for seven years before he began teaching. He has written widely and made a number of presentations on First Amendment topics. *Mass Communication Law in Virginia* is his third book. He and his wife, Roselynn, an art teacher, have three sons.

Mass Communication Law in Virginia